D1058208

"The transformation of the Worldwide Church of God represents a unique phenomenon in church history. As such it warrants careful documentation and in-depth reflection, especially from an insider's perspective. Mike Feazell is well qualified for that challenging task as one who has for many years been part of the leadership core of that church. His account is deeply moving, reflecting his personal struggles; refreshingly honest in dealing not only with the theological issues but the pastoral implications for the leaders and members who were traumatized by the changes; and theologically perceptive in exploring the changes in his church's key doctrines. I believe that *The Liberation of the Worldwide Church of God* is destined to become a standard work, which church historians and religious sociologists will continue to consult for years to come."

—EDDIE GIBBS
School of Theology,
Fuller Theological Seminary

What Others Are Saying About the Worldwide Church of God

"I have met with the leadership of the church, and without reservation consider them brothers in Christ. I am profoundly moved by their testimonies of what God has done for them personally and in the movement. These people have led the most courageous, inspiring, and Christ-centered movement into biblical Christianity that I have ever seen."

—Richard Mouw
President, Fuller Theological Seminary

"This is the most astonishing change that I have ever seen or heard of in any religious group, for which, for one, praise God."

—D. James Kennedy
Coral Ridge Presbyterian Church
Fort Lauderdale, Florida

"Never before in the history of Christianity has there been such a complete move to orthodox Christianity by an unorthodox fringe church."

—Ruth Tucker
Associate Professor
Calvin Theological Seminary

Quotations from "From the Fringe to the Fold," by Ruth Tucker (*Christianity Today*, July 15, 1996).

THE LIBERATION
of the WORLDWIDE
CHURCH *of* GOD

THE LIBERATION
of the WORLDWIDE
CHURCH *of* GOD

J. Michael Feazell

Executive Editor, *Plain Truth* Magazine

GRAND RAPIDS, MICHIGAN 49530

We want to hear from you. Please send your comments about this book to us in care of the address below. Thank you.

Zondervan
Grand Rapids, Michigan 49530
www.zondervan.com

ZONDERVAN™

The Liberation of the Worldwide Church of God
Copyright © 2001 by J. Michael Feazell
Requests for information should be addressed to:

Zondervan, Grand Rapids, Michigan 49530

Library of Congress Cataloging-in-Publication Data
Feazell, J. Michael.
    The liberation of the Worldwide Church of God : the remarkable story of a cult's journey from deception to truth / J. Michael Feazell.
       p.   cm.
    Includes bibliographical references (p.).
    ISBN 0–310–23858–7 (hardcover)
    1. Worldwide Church of God.   2. Armstrong, Herbert W.   I. Title.
BX6178.A73 F43 2001
289.9—dc21   2001023552

This edition printed on acid-free paper.

Interior design by Melissa Elenbaas

Printed in the United States of America

---

01 02 03 04 05 06 07 08 /❖ DC/ 10 9 8 7 6 5 4 3 2 1

To Victoria
Wife, companion, friend

"Oh, thank GOD—he's so good!
His love never runs out.
All of you set free by GOD, tell the world!
Tell how he freed you from oppression,
Then rounded you up from all over the place,
From the four winds, from the seven seas."

PSALM 107:1–3 THE MESSAGE

CONTENTS

PREFACE

THE AMAZING CHANGES IN the Worldwide Church of God have prompted many Christians to ask, "How did all this begin?"

I have been asked this question scores of times, but I have to pause and reflect anew every time I hear it. How did all this begin? I cannot point to a single starting place either for the transformation of the Worldwide Church of God or for myself. I cannot isolate a particular moment, a particular place, or a particular thought. Many things came together like tiny brooks and rivulets, bubbling up from here and there and nowhere in particular but little by little joining with others and growing steadily to form larger streams and finally cascading together into a mighty river.

How did all this begin? It began in the hearts of men and women who heard the voice of their Savior. It began in the testimony of Scripture. It began in the pain and frustration of unforgiving moralism. It began in the agonizing disillusionment that comes from failed predictions and fallen heroes. It began in the idealism of youth and the simple wisdom of old age. It began when the angel spoke the timeless words of hope and redemption to the shepherds: "Today in the town of David a Savior has been born to you. He is Christ the Lord."

Some readers may feel that my approach in this book has an "edge." Perhaps it does, but that is not my intent. I am presenting what I believe to be an honest assessment, as unbiased as I am able to give, of what the Worldwide Church of God was, why I believe it needed to change, how the Holy Spirit led that change to take place, and what I hope all Christian churches can learn from our experience. Some may feel that I am disrespectful to Herbert Armstrong. Some may feel I am too respectful. I can only say that I have tried to be honest and fair.

The Liberation of the Worldwide Church of God is not only a remarkable story of the doctrinal transformation of a highly influential Christian sect—considered by many to be a cult—but also the story of a spiritual journey from the prison of soul-crippling legalism into the liberating joy and rest of eternal salvation.

HISTORY IN THE MAKING

The Worldwide Church of God made evangelical history in the early 1990s with its leadership-driven abandonment of the unorthodox doctrines of its founder, renowned radio and television evangelist Herbert W. Armstrong. The radical changes in the small, Pasadena-based Christian denomination have been heralded by mainstream Christian leaders as "miraculous," "astounding," and "unprecedented." No other Christian church in our modern experience has rejected its founding sectarian roots in a return to the essentials of historical Christian doctrinal orthodoxy.

It is my hope that *The Liberation of the Worldwide Church of God* will be of help to members of the Worldwide Church of God in understanding what has happened to our church historically, doctrinally, and spiritually, and that it will offer encouragement to the church to continue wisely in the future. I pray that this book might also motivate leaders and members of any Christian church to vigilance in promoting and encouraging careful theological reflection coupled with authentic spiritual formation. It is my further prayer that the book may be of value to Christian leaders as a tool to help them recognize and avoid the spiritual traps and excesses that plagued Armstrongism.

All material in this book regarding the Worldwide Church of God is drawn from extensive textual research of the published literature of the church, from oral history, and from more than forty years of personal experience and contacts in the church— first, as a graduate of the church's grade school, high school, and college; then as an ordained minister and a denominational executive in the church for more than twenty years. This study also draws upon my intimate personal involvement with the process of doctrinal transformation that took place in the Worldwide Church of God. As executive assistant and senior editorial advisor to Joseph Tkach Sr., Herbert Armstrong's personally chosen successor, I was afforded a unique perspective into the church and a firsthand role in its transformation.

ACKNOWLEDGMENTS

W‍ERE IT NOT FOR the gentle reassurance and the confidence shown in me by my professors at Azusa Pacific University, this project would not have been undertaken. I am especially grateful for the infectious enthusiasm and can-do spirit of Dr. Earl Grant, associate dean of the C. P. Haggard Graduate School of Theology. Dr. Richard Foster enriched my vision of the kingdom of God and offered much encouragement as the first portions of this book took shape. Dr. Eddie Gibbs's insightful suggestions and patient, diligent, and gracious manner in critiquing my work were invaluable.

I cannot say enough about the patient and careful work of my editor at Zondervan, Jim Ruark, whose masterful editor's pen was simply invaluable. Jim's encouragement and kind spirit were as important to my work as his marvelous editorial skills.

I must also thank three of my colleagues in the Worldwide Church of God. Ralph Orr, former coordinator of in-service pastoral training, and Dan Rogers, U.S. superintendent of ministers, gave me several helpful editorial suggestions during early drafts. Michael Morrison, editorial supervisor for the church, was kind enough to give my final manuscript a careful review and provided numerous excellent suggestions that sharpened the final product.

I am grateful to John and Micki McKenna for their constant stream of encouragement, to Barb Edwards for her help with numerous clerical details, and to C. S. Lewis, Madeleine L'Engle, and Henri Nouwen, whose blessed inspirational writings carried me through many painful times.

Most of all, I am deeply indebted to my wife, Victoria, and to my children, Jeff, Liz, and Chris, for their support and encouragement, through whom I have learned much about the grace of God.

PROLOGUE

RULES AND REGULATIONS OF "God's true church" took center stage in my life from the first day I toured the Ambassador College campus in Pasadena, California. It was 1957, I was six years old, and my family had moved from Louisiana to California to allow me to attend "God's school," the Worldwide Church of God Imperial Grade and High School. As my uncle, Paul Smith, himself a graduate of "God's college" and a teacher at the school, led the family around the immaculate campus, I found myself awestruck with the elegance and sheer beauty of "God's headquarters on earth."

As I write these words, I am still swept with strange feelings of nostalgia for the sense of "something great" that seemed to flood over me during that first encounter with Herbert Armstrong's center of operations.

As we made our way up one of the elegant Ambassador walkways, my six-year-old eyes noticed a little sign planted in the largest, most beautiful and lush lawn I had ever seen. Brand new at reading, I sounded out the words for my family: "Keep off the Grass."

"What does that mean?" I asked my uncle. It was incomprehensible to this Louisiana boy that grass could exist for anything other than getting *on*.

"This is a very special kind of grass," Uncle Paul explained. "In fact, it's really not grass at all. It's called *dichondra*. And it is very expensive and very fragile, so Mr. Armstrong doesn't want anyone to walk on it. That's how we can keep it looking so beautiful."

I immediately saw the reason for the rule, and I made it my lifelong policy to never walk on Ambassador's magnificent carpets of green. At the same time, though, I felt it was a colossal shame that what seemed to me to be the most fantastic lawns in the world could only be looked at and not romped on.

That is what legalism does to people. It can create the illusion of something wonderful. But something that can never become what it was meant to be is not, in the end, wonderful. Maybe it is better than nothing, but it is still at best only a hollow shell. And until the liberating roar of Aslan shatters it into the worthless dust it is, legalism, ironically, imprisons its victims in a confounding dungeon of smug anxiety and self-satisfied frustration.

Lawns, to be true lawns, need boys and girls to play on them. Human beings, to be the true persons God made them to be, need at their center the heart of God expressing itself through love. Following the rules does not produce a relationship of love. Condemning others who do not keep the rules the way you think they ought to be kept does not produce a relationship of love. A relationship of love is based on knowing and loving a *person*, not on knowing and loving a set of rules.

These lessons would be long in coming to the Worldwide Church of God and to me. Many years and many experiences would set the stage for a miraculous work of grace, a liberation that no one associated with Herbert Armstrong's church in those early years would ever have imagined.

A CRACK IN THE DAM

A S HAS BEEN SAID, the Church is like Noah's ark," I read aloud, quoting from Charles Colson's *The Body*. "The stench inside would be unbearable if it weren't for the storm outside."[1] The group laughed. I continued: "And as imperfect and even repugnant as we find it at times, we need to acknowledge that it is through this church of fact that truth is being proclaimed and portrayed." As I read, I hoped Colson's words might find fertile soil in my audience:

> Not always clearly; not always unequivocally. I cringe when I hear a church leader does some dumb or dreadful thing. I want to scream that the National Council of Churches isn't speaking for me (and it isn't). But somehow through all of the muddle, the message is kept alive. People often come to church for all the wrong reasons, but God touches them, and nearly apostate churches are resurrected. God does it, using us just as we are.

I struggled to control my trembling voice. God had touched *our* church. He had touched *me*. His grace had come upon us completely unannounced, and he had transformed our hearts before we even knew what was happening. I read on: "The church of fact is always struggling to conform to the church of faith, and the Christian must live in the midst of this tension—a faithful part of the universal and the particular, of the visible and invisible, of the faith and the fact."

I fought back the tears. So many thoughts flooded my mind. God loved us in spite of our confusion and doctrinal error. He had come to our church and redeemed us in spite of our self-righteousness, our exclusivity, and our tendency to be judgmental.

How far we have come, I thought. The very fact I could be reading to this group from Colson, a *Protestant*, was a miracle. The fact that many of these ministers and wives were ready to hear Colson's insights was a miracle. And the fact that Colson's next words had been so powerfully played out in this very group was also a miracle:

> Admittedly, the pettiness and failures, the division and discord, can be disheartening at times. What a sorry mess we mortals often make of things in the name of the church! But our comfort comes from God's promise that He will build His church—sometimes in extraordinary ways.

The group was a conference of pastors of the Worldwide Church of God. And the miracle was the amazing story of the Holy Spirit's liberating and transforming work in the renowned church, called a cult by some, founded by media evangelist Herbert W. Armstrong.

"MR. ARMSTRONG DIED THIS MORNING"

The story had begun some ten years earlier on January 16, 1986, at about 7:30 in the morning. I was about to leave for work when the phone rang. My wife, Victoria, answered, exchanged a few words with the caller, and gave the phone to me.

"It's Mr. Tkach," she said.

Joseph W. Tkach Sr. was my boss. I had known him since 1966. I was sixteen when his employer, the Worldwide Church of God, transferred his family from Chicago to Pasadena, California. As an ordained minister, he had been brought to Pasadena to take classes in the denomination's Ambassador College and to serve in the Los Angeles congregation. His son Joe and I were in tenth grade, and before long we were close friends.

Now, twenty years later, the senior Tkach was director of church administration for the denomination, and I was his executive assistant. He was also 93-year-old Herbert Armstrong's personally chosen successor.

"Mr. Armstrong died this morning," he told me. His voice was solemn and shaky. "I have been calling the Council of Elders. We will need to notify the field ministers and the news media. I'll see you at the office."

Tkach, alternating with Armstrong's aide, Aaron Dean, and a nursing staff, had for weeks been spending nearly every evening, night, and early morning with the ailing Armstrong in the pastor general's residence on the Ambassador College campus in Pasadena. He kept Armstrong company, helped him with personal needs, and listened to his advice and instructions. He was there the morning Armstrong died.

Tkach had grown close to Herbert Armstrong during the final year of Armstrong's life. The aging Armstrong had come to the point where, he told Tkach and others, he felt he could trust no one. "I know you will take good care of the ministry," he told him. Tkach recounted to me many times how much Armstrong appreciated his being there. Armstrong had appointed Tkach to succeed him as president and pastor general of the church, and he wanted to be sure he had passed on all the insight he could during his final weeks and days.

"I can't fill his shoes. But, Father, I aim to walk in his footsteps," Tkach prayed at the special church headquarters employee meeting the morning of Armstrong's death. The church was numb, but the church was not shaken. "The transition was so smooth," I heard again and again from ministers and members.

Sermons were given about Joshua following in Moses' foot-steps. "Be strong and of good courage," pastors and members were telling Tkach, echoing Yahweh's words to Joshua after Moses' death.

Upon assuming his new role as president and pastor general of the Worldwide Church of God, Tkach asked me to continue in the role of his executive assistant. I was glad to serve. I wanted to help him see that the teachings of Herbert Armstrong were maintained and that the church would "make herself ready" for the return of Christ. Little did I know what lay ahead.

THE JOURNEY BEGINS

When Herbert Armstrong died, my entire focus was to help Joseph Tkach Sr. maintain Armstrong's teachings and ministry. If anything needed to be changed, I believed, it would only be details.

Within weeks, however, the first challenge was raised to Armstrong's presumed absolute insight on the Scriptures. Mark Kaplan, an Ambassador College[2] professor of Hebrew, raised a question about Armstrong's dogmatic teaching that the children of Israel did not depart from Egypt on the same night as they ate the Passover meal but on the next night.

I distributed Kaplan's papers to the members of the Council of Elders, and the consensus was that Kaplan was right. The pre-ponderance of scriptural evidence lay in favor of the millennia-old Jewish viewpoint (what a surprise!).

The crack was in the dam. Armstrong was wrong about a point he had taught with particular force and dogmatism. Tkach decided that the best course of action was to delete the offend-ing section from the church booklet about the annual holy days and officially inform the pastors that the issue is merely histor-ical, not doctrinal, and therefore of no consequence.

Most pastors accepted the action, but there was something uneasy about the whole thing. Armstrong had been so dogmatic on the issue, using his characteristic capital letters, italics, and underlining to make his point.

Now Tkach, holding the office of "God's apostle," the only person on earth through whom God brings doctrine into his church, had neatly thrown out a dogmatic Armstrong teaching. How can one "God's only true apostle" change the teaching of the other "God's only true apostle"?

Small or "merely historical" as this particular point may have been, later changes would raise the larger question: How can Tkach have the authority to change Armstrong's teaching? And then the conundrum: If Armstrong was wrong about that, then could he have been wrong about appointing Tkach? And worse, but still unthinkable at this early stage: If Armstrong really *was* wrong about something he felt God had revealed to him, how could he have called himself "God's only true apostle"?

SPOKESMAN CLUB MANUAL

The next lesson in coming to see Armstrongism in a new light was the revision of the church's Spokesman Club manual. The Spokesman Club manual had been the mainstay of the men's discipleship experience for decades. Based on the rules of the Toastmaster's Club, the Spokesman Club was a leadership training ground for Worldwide Church of God (WCG) men. A series of speech assignments, designed to improve communication skills and encourage personal growth and leadership, were outlined in the manual.

One of Tkach's first goals was to dismantle the authoritarian approach to government in the church, which meant that the Spokesman Club manual needed revision on two counts: its authoritarian style, and its hyperbolic language that promised near perfection and amazing success to anyone who followed its rules carefully. Setting out to edit the manual was an eye-opening lesson in where we had been as a church. I had never really analyzed our church literature with the eye of a critic.

Now it was my job to make sure our literature did not promote authoritarianism and that all content was accurate and biblically defensible. I really had no thought at all about doctrine at this point. My assumption was that Herbert Armstrong was correct on every important doctrinal issue. I pitied those poor souls who could not understand the difference between important doctrine and mere "semantical issues."

As we revised the Spokesman Club manual, our booklet editor, Ronald D. Kelly (now church controller), remarked, "I never realized how these things sounded before." That is not surprising. We had always tended to read the church's literature as *prima facie* true—already believing its truth and authority before we even began reading it. Now for the first time we were reading for the specific purpose of editing its accuracy. The results were disconcerting, to say the least. As we finished each booklet, we were almost afraid to start on the next.

We did not choose the order of booklets to revise. That was purely a function of inventory. As booklets ran out of stock and came up for reprinting, they had to be reviewed. It seemed that every time we reviewed a booklet, we found serious problems with it. And even then, for the first few years, our revisions did not go deep enough. Some booklets, like *The Missing Dimension in Sex*, underwent major revision every time it came up for reprinting as our understanding increased. Finally, it had to be removed from inventory, a fate that eventually befell every one of the more than eighty booklets the Worldwide Church of God was regularly mailing out in 1986.

As doctrinal problems became more apparent, however, even some in-stock booklets had to be removed from inventory. That was the case with Armstrong's powerful attack on Protestant Christianity, *Just What Do You Mean—Born Again?*

GREEK WORDS, ENGLISH WORDS

Herbert Armstrong and scholarship did not mix well. He continually ridiculed what he branded as "this world's degrees,"

"so-called higher education," and people who "fancied themselves as scholars." He encouraged church members not to send
their children to the colleges and universities of "this world," but
only to the church's Ambassador College. Many of Armstrong's
doctrinal errors sprang directly from his ignorance of biblical
scholarship and sound methods of biblical interpretation.

Early in 1987 I received a memo from Kyriakos Stavrinides,
a church minister and professor of classics and Greek at Ambassador College, citing major problems with Armstrong's booklet
Just What Do You Mean—Born Again? My first reaction was to
roll my eyes and mumble, "Here we go again." I reviewed the
memo with Joseph Tkach Sr., and at Tkach's request went to discuss it with Stavrinides.

Armstrong taught that Christians are not finally "born again"
until they receive glorified bodies at the resurrection. Until then,
Armstrong asserted, Christians are only "begotten," which he
took to mean "merely conceived" but not yet born. Stavrinides
explained that the Greek word transliterated *gennao* does mean
"begotten," as Herbert Armstrong taught. But contrary to Armstrong's belief, the English word *begotten* does not mean "conceived." Rather, the word *begotten* refers to live birth. In this case,
Armstrong's confusion lay in his misunderstanding of 400-year-
old King James English, not in the meaning of the Greek word.
On this simple mistake of English grammar, Herbert Armstrong
had built the entire edifice of his doctrine that "you are not
finally born again until the resurrection."

It was not just the false doctrine that was so rankling. It was
Armstrong's attitude about it and his presentation of it. His
"rightness" on this point gave him, he believed, the right to condemn any who disagreed with him as "falsely so-called Christians" who were deceived by the devil. Armstrong's challenges to
the "professing" Christian world were boldly emphasized by his
characteristic advertising font styles:

> WHY cannot people understand? It's hard to believe, but
> YOUR BIBLE says that *this whole world* is DECEIVED!

Incredible though it seems, that is true!

Yes, even the clergy![3]

All the clergy except Armstrong, that is. This is what happens when a person, in his or her own mind, becomes "God's special representative." I have to warn any Christian—if the leader of your church or group begins to make noise about being God's special mouthpiece, or the "only one" preaching some particular message or some particular way, then my advice to you is to move on down the road.

DEPRESSION AND DISCOURAGEMENT

By early 1989, I had reached a low point both emotionally and spiritually. I was being confronted with error after error in Armstrong's theology. Doctrinal and theological questions were continually being posed to the church administration department and to the pastor general's office from church ministers and members. As Tkach Sr. and I struggled to respond to these questions with scriptural honesty and integrity, I was beginning to realize that the Worldwide Church of God was not, after all, the "one and only true church" and that Herbert Armstrong was not God's only true servant on earth.

There was never a problem discussing these issues openly with Joseph Tkach Sr. Still, even though he put a great deal of trust in me as his primary assistant, he nevertheless received a free flow of input from a great many people besides me in the administration of the church, and rightly so. He could not help but be at least somewhat influenced by the grave concerns expressed to him about me and my "liberal ideas" by longtime ministers who feared the "dangerous direction" the doctrinal changes were going. By early 1989, changes had already taken place in the church's doctrines regarding the use of the medical profession, women's use of cosmetics, and celebration of birthdays. These changes, which were already traumatic enough for the 150,000-member church, as well as the inevitable rumors of more to come, began to create a sense that the floodgates were about to be opened.

"You have got to stop listening to Mike Feazell," Tkach Sr. was often warned. "Mike is trying to get you to destroy everything God did through Herbert Armstrong. Mike is a very dangerous influence on you. You have to get rid of him," was the impassioned plea that became a familiar tune to Tkach Sr.'s ears. (Later, the circle of "dangerous liberal conspirators" expanded to include booklet editor Greg Albrecht, media operations director Bernie Schnippert, classics professor Kyriakos Stavrinides, and church administration director Joe Tkach Jr.—the "gang of five.")

Getting to the place where I felt I could trust no one with these heart-level issues, and feeling generally friendless, depressed, and thoroughly discouraged, I took an offered opportunity to accompany Donald Ward, then president of Ambassador College, on an inspection visit to Ambassador Foundation's humanitarian projects staffed by Ambassador College students in the Hashemite Kingdom of Jordan. I hoped the trip would provide me some time to pray, reflect, and get some perspective.

As I sat on the plane, my thoughts went everywhere. How could the church have lied to me all these years? I felt taken advantage of, spiritually and emotionally raped. It seemed as though my life had been robbed from me. I could have gone to a state college and had a real career and maybe even been a real Christian. I was angry. I was confused. I was depressed. And I was disgusted with the seductive assault on the true gospel waged by Herbert Armstrong's "one and only true church." I prayed earnestly for God to show me his clear path for my life and to give me peace of heart.

Looking back, I see that God answers such prayers, but not often in the ways we desire or expect. He knows what we need. We only know what we *want*. As it turns out, God has given me just enough peace of heart to know he is still there, and just enough assurance of his path for me to know that I can always trust him with my life—even though I rarely know where he is taking it.

GRADUATE SCHOOL

Charles Wallace Davis, my assistant from 1990 to 1993, was a godsend. A young man of faith, peace, and honesty, C. W., as he liked to be called, had been recommended to me by Donald Ward, whom he had served as a faculty assistant during his senior year at Ambassador College. C. W. made a wonderful assistant. He gave me much needed emotional support and encouragement, and set a simple, steadfast example of trusting God and waiting patiently for God to act.

At Donald Ward's recommendation, C. W. and I began attending the C. P. Haggard Graduate School of Theology at Azusa Pacific University in the fall of 1990. Dr. Earl Grant, associate dean of the graduate school, met and prayed with C. W. and me in late summer that year. To my knowledge, he was the first Christian leader who offered support and encouragement to the Worldwide Church of God as the denomination's transformation was getting under way. From the day of our first meeting, Earl has been a true Christian brother and friend.

Dr. Grant's gracious acceptance of our fledgling desires for sound Christian education and his heartfelt prayer for God's blessing on us and our denomination was characteristic of the reception we received from the faculty and administration of the graduate school. They never interfered. They never pushed. They never tried to change us or "convert" us. They simply taught the Bible in all the joy and enthusiasm the Lord provides those who love him, and they did it at a time when no other Christian graduate school would even consider admitting us. Perhaps more than anything else, their example of Christian love in being willing to risk their reputation to serve people who were considered by other Christians to be a cult will always be an inspiration to me—and a characteristic I pray our fellowship will be able to replicate and teach as the Lord wills.

DOCTRINAL DISCUSSION GROUP

In late 1989 I approached Joseph Tkach Sr. with the idea of forming a doctrinal discussion team that would create a formal statement of beliefs for the Worldwide Church of God as well as give formal review to the many challenges we were receiving to Herbert Armstrong's doctrines. Tkach gave his approval, appointed thirteen senior ministers and faculty members to the team, and assigned me to chair it. We had to carefully avoid the term "doctrinal committee" because that still carried sinister overtones from the days when Armstrong condemned the "setting of doctrine in the church" by anyone but "God's specially called and chosen apostle" (that is, Armstrong himself). Calling ourselves the "Doctrinal Manual Group," we drafted the following statements of purpose and began meeting weekly in January 1990:

1. To ensure that the doctrinal theology as taught in the classes of Ambassador College and the tenets of belief and doctrine as taught in the Worldwide Church of God are consistent between the two entities.
2. To provide a structured, yet open, forum in which doctrinal matters can be raised and discussed to the end that further doctrinal growth and refinement will occur.
3. To provide a source of academic theological counsel to the pastor general of the Church.[4]

Instructions encouraged free discussion among the members of the team:

> Most of the materials you receive will be in draft form, prepared in the Editorial department. Please rewrite sections you feel need to be rewritten. Also, the confidential nature of this work enables you to be as candid as you

wish to be. Mr. Tkach's goal is that we look to God to lead us into all truth. The Church is not to preserve traditional understanding for the sake of preserving it. Nor is the Church to discard traditional understanding for the sake of discarding it. We want to state the Church's understanding in as clear and as complete terms as we are able. In areas where members of the group feel the Church's current understanding may need revision, recommendations on such proposed revisions will be given to Mr. Tkach as a part of the group's function.

Mr. Tkach will review all observations and recommendations of the group and make all final decisions regarding the manual and other statements. He will be presented with all points of view among the group that do not agree with the general consensus. Therefore, please do not hold back your true feelings.[5]

UP THE CREEK WITHOUT A PADDLE

The path of working through doctrinal issues was a rocky one. One member of the panel, a longtime minister and a man of solid Christian character and a pure heart, said quite honestly, "I feel like I'm up the creek without a paddle." And he was. His training at Armstrong's Ambassador College had not even remotely prepared him for such discussions. His reading in the intervening years had included few, if any, books by Christian scholars about Christian doctrine, Christian history, or Christian theology. He was, in fact, just as we all had been, up the creek without a paddle.

The discussions about the doctrine of the Trinity were as fascinating as they were frustrating and tedious. During one discussion about the anthropomorphic references to God in the Old Testament, a panel member asked, "What does 'figurative' mean?" What were we supposed to say to that? It is a sad day when a senior member of a church's doctrinal review team doesn't know the difference between figurative and literal.

"Well," Kyriakos Stavrinides began to explain in his characteristically patient manner, "when a word or expression is used in a figurative sense, it is painting a picture of a reality that cannot adequately be described in literal terms."

"But why don't we just take the Bible for what it says?" was the sincere response.

"When the Bible uses figurative language, that *is* what the Bible is saying," I offered in response. "Figurative language doesn't imply that the statement is less true. It simply means that the statement is to be understood figuratively, not literally. In other words, it is a true statement, and it is to be understood figuratively, not literally."

"I'm totally lost. I guess I just don't understand how something that isn't real can be true."

"Let me give an illustration," Stavrinides offered. "If I say to my wife, 'You are a rose,' I have made a true statement, and I really mean what I say. She is lovely and pleasing, just as a rose is lovely and pleasing, though in different specific ways. I do not mean she is literally a rose. I mean that there are certain important characteristics of a rose that my wife shares. Or we might say, 'Life is a river.' And we mean what we say. We might mean that just as a river flows down the riverbed, so life's moments flow toward their conclusion. But we do not mean that life is literally billions of gallons of water moving across an indention in the landscape. What we say is no less real because it is figurative."

"Well, I just don't get it. It seems to me you can just call something figurative any time you don't want to believe it. How can you tell the difference? I say something means what it says, and you say it's figurative. So I guess we disagree."

Stavrinides continued to explain patiently the value and importance of figurative language in the Bible. It was helpful for some and a complete fog for others.

Another panel member seemed only to be able to think in terms of what Herbert Armstrong had written or said. He began nearly every comment with: "Mr. Herbert W. Armstrong said . . ." or "I have here Mr. Herbert W. Armstrong's article on . . . " or "On page such and such of *Mystery of the Ages,* Mr. Herbert W. Armstrong wrote. . . ." To him and to thousands like him in the Worldwide Church of God, Armstrong was God's man, and God had revealed through Armstrong everything the church needed to know. To call Armstrong's revelations into question was tantamount to the spirit of antichrist.

Herbert W. Armstrong preaching to the Pasadena congregation of the Worldwide Church of God in Ambassador Auditorium.

Joseph W. Tkach Sr., Herbert W. Armstrong's successor as pastor general.

A VOICE IN THE WILDERNESS

THE MINISTRY OF HERBERT W. Armstrong began in 1931 after his ordination by the Oregon Conference of the Church of God (Seventh Day), a small Sabbatarian sect founded in the wake of William Miller's prophetic failure of 1844. Armstrong, a gifted advertising man, had been brought into contact with the Sabbatarians by his wife, Loma, who had become convinced by a neighbor that observance of the Saturday Sabbath was a binding law for Christians. In the fall of 1926, Armstrong, embarrassed by his wife's "fanaticism,"[1] set out to prove her wrong. The result of his "six months of virtual night-and-day, seven-day-a-week study and research"[2] at the Portland Public Library was his own conversion to Sabbatarianism and his personal sense of call to Christian ministry.

SPECIAL CALLING

At first Herbert Armstrong's ministry looked similar to any Christian ministry. Using typical tent-campaign techniques, he began preaching the gospel (with a strong Sabbatarian bent) in the Eugene and Portland areas. Early in his studies, however, Armstrong came into contact with the British-Israelism theories of J. H. Allen.[3] Inexorably influenced by this "lost"[4] teaching, Armstrong began to feel that he was specially chosen by God to proclaim an end-time warning message to the United States and to the whole world, a message he came to call the "end-time Elijah" warning message, in reference to the prophecy of Malachi 4:5–6.[5] This conviction led him to begin a local radio and publishing ministry, which he intended to expand to the whole world as support grew.

Armstrong's radio program, *The World Tomorrow*, focused on the growing likelihood of war in Europe, then began covering the war itself. He connected his British-Israel ideas to the prophecies of Ezekiel, proclaiming that Hitler's Germany would win the war and attack the United States. The fall of the United States to the Nazis would fulfill the prophecies about Israel's punishment at the hands of the Beast of Revelation, which he connected with Assyria of Ezekiel's prophecies and with an end-time resurrection of the Holy Roman Empire.

After the Allied victory over the Axis powers in World War II, Armstrong began proclaiming a final "resurrection" of the "European beast power," perhaps led by Hitler himself, whom Armstrong suggested might not be dead at all, but in hiding, waiting to reappear as a counterfeit "resurrected" Savior.[6] One way or another, the modern-day descendants of the lost ten tribes of Israel, Armstrong trumpeted, would soon be severely punished by God at the hands of a united European beast power for its sins, primarily those of abandoning Sabbath and holy day observance.[7]

As Armstrong's ministry grew, he and his followers became increasingly convinced of his special calling. First, his church was incorporated as the Radio Church of God, a name derived from the fact that Armstrong was pastoring his flock over the airwaves. Later, the church name was changed to Worldwide Church of God, a reflection of Armstrong's belief that his was the "only true church" and that he alone was commissioned to preach the gospel in all the world to the last generation before the return of Christ.

Armstrong's message combined his prophetic, Sabbatarian, and holy day theories with a general Holiness Christian tradition. Except for his aberrant dogmas on the Trinity, old covenant laws, and interpretation of prophecy, Armstrong's church shared many characteristics of American fundamentalism. Interestingly, while Armstrong's theology called for radical obedience to those elements of the old covenant he deemed binding on Christians, namely Saturday Sabbath, holy days, and meat laws, he took a more "balanced" perspective on what he considered nonessential issues of Christian behavior, such as drinking alcohol (he taught moderation), playing cards, movies, dancing, and mixed swimming. He took a decisively negative stance on pharmaceuticals, women's makeup, tobacco, interracial marriage, birthday celebration, and celebration of what he deemed "pagan" holidays, such as Easter, Christmas, Halloween, and Valentine's Day.

ARBITER OF DOCTRINE

Once Armstrong had established Ambassador College in Pasadena, California, in 1947 to train ministers for his rapidly growing church, the dogmatism skyrocketed. Surrounded by young, devoted admirers, passionate about their special call to assist him in the "most important work on the face of the earth," Armstrong's opinion of himself and his ministry began to take on messianic proportions. His autobiography illustrates the battle lines between his sense of the "true church" (the one he founded) and every other Christian church:

> I had been astounded to learn that the BIBLE teaches truths diametrically opposite to the teachings of the large and popular churches and denominations today. I saw in the Bible the real MISSION of God's true Church. But these churches, today, were *not* carrying on the real work and mission of Christ.
>
> The SOURCE of their beliefs and practice was *not* the Bible, but paganism! There was no recognizable comparison between them and the original TRUE Church I found described in Acts and other New Testament books. Yet *somewhere there had to exist today* that spiritual organ-

ism in which Christ actually dwelt—a church empowered by His Spirit—acting as His instrument—carrying
out His Commission.

But where?

I was still to be some years in finding the answer.

I still had to sift out the real truth *a doctrine at a time*.[8]

Armstrong continued his sifting process without, of course, the
discipline of subjecting his ideas to the broader witness of Christian history, and he became increasingly convinced that he was the
only true apostle and arbiter of doctrine on earth. Without accountability to the broader body of Christ, Armstrong's undisciplined
interpretation of Scripture naturally led to doctrinal heresy.

Ironically, Armstrong acknowledged the importance of testing one's personal interpretations of Scripture against the consensual witness of the church:

But, exciting as these new truths were to me, I realized
fully I was *new* in the truth—a novice spiritually—a "babe
in Christ." I deemed it wise to have this newly discovered
truth about the day of the resurrection verified by others
more experienced in Biblical understanding than I.[9]

In the case cited, however, Armstrong's personal practice of
the principle to which he accedes was to share his research with
only one lay Christian, who discussed it with his pastor, and the
two of them could not refute Armstrong's conclusions.[10] His
own illustration demonstrates that Armstrong was unable to
give more than lip service to the idea of consensual witness. The
result was predictable. Armstrong not only held onto his "new
truths," but he also convinced himself that he had truly sub-
jected them to the scrutiny of the wider body of Christ.

Not surprisingly, Armstrong's willingness to place his personal "discoveries" above the historical witness of the Spirit in
the church eventually led him to scrap altogether the need for
consensual witness.

GOD'S FAITHFUL

To Armstrong and his followers, WCG distinctives became the tests of the "one and only true church." Primary distinctives included the following:

- Observance of the seventh-day Sabbath and annual Israelite holy days
- A doctrine of the modern identity of the "lost ten tribes"
- A gospel centering on the return of Christ and a future millennium on earth
- Three tithes: one for the work of the church, one for personal expenses at the required annual festivals, and one every third and sixth year of a seven-year cycle for the widows and the poor
- Adherence to the Old Testament unclean meat laws
- Rejection of the doctrines of the immortal soul and hell
- Rejection of Trinitarianism
- Avoidance of traditional Christian festivals
- Avoidance of voting and military service
- Avoidance of most forms of medical care
- A unique premillennial triple-resurrection schema
- Major emphasis on mass-media ministry
- The belief that the Worldwide Church of God was the only true Christian church and that Herbert Armstrong was specially raised up and inspired by God to be the "Elijah to come" who would "restore all things," including right doctrine, in preparation for the return of Christ

The bottom line: Only those who were baptized members of the Worldwide Church of God were considered God's faithful. *The Ambassador College Bible Correspondence Course*, Armstrong's chief educational tool, put it this way:

As the terms of the New Covenant are now part of the Savior's Testament—His *Will*—THE *TRUE* CHURCH of God today IS THE EXECUTOR OR ADMINISTRA-

TOR OF THIS WILL by which one may obtain the Holy Spirit OF ENTRANCE INTO GOD'S KINGDOM. Christ FOUNDED His Church FOR THIS PURPOSE. The very fact that we know *why* this Will was made—its true intent and purpose—together with proof we are the *true* Church formed for executing this Will, makes *us* its executors! We are the ones who possess the "keys" today. God's true Church is NOT the SHOUTING, SENSE-LESS "PENTECOSTAL-TYPE" OF CHURCH. God's Spirit is "the Spirit of a sound mind," in A SOUND CHURCH WHICH HAS the KEYS OF THE KING-DOM. . . . Do *not* make the FATAL MISTAKE of attempting to *COVENANT* with God THROUGH THE *WRONG* CHURCH.

Remember that after you are begotten, you must *grow.* IF you CHOOSE the *WRONG* CHURCH through which to covenant with God, you will BE FED the *WRONG* SPIRITUAL FOOD. You will then *DIE SPIRI-TUALLY* if you are fed this wrong spiritual food.

And then you CANNOT BE BORN AGAIN at Christ's soon-coming!

And finally, keep always in mind that God's final *warn-ing* message *to all the earth* must be carried by *radio.* That is the only human force *powerful* enough to do it! That's why THIS WORK is CALLED THE *RADIO* CHURCH OF GOD ["Radio" was eventually dropped for "World-wide."].[11]

TACKLING NOMINALISM

Inherent in this radically judgmental and self-enamored per-spective was Armstrong's concept of a nationwide problem of nominal Christianity. A 1963 church booklet explained Arm-strong's viewpoint on the role of biblical law in American Chris-tian churches:

But Mr. Armstrong's Sunday school days had taught him that there are NO WORKS to salvation—God's Law was DONE AWAY. To him, religion had not been a WAY OF LIFE, but a mere BELIEF—an acceptance of the FACTS of God's existence, Christ's virgin birth, the efficacy of Christ's shed blood. Religion, to him, had been a Sunday morning hour-and-a-half at church (which he had neglected for some 15 or 16 years)—and had nothing to do with how he lived the rest of the week.[12]

Armstrong passionately taught that Christianity is to be "a way of life."[13] He was right to condemn cheap grace, easy belief, and an empty profession of faith. The likes of Bonhoeffer, Tozer, and Merton would agree with Armstrong's denunciation of nominal Christianity. But sadly, Armstrong's solution proved to be equally as empty and devoid of Spirit life as the problem itself.

Eddie Gibbs cites ten common elements that promote nominality in the life of a local church:

1. The congregation has never had the Gospel clearly presented in the power of the Holy Spirit.
2. The authority of the Bible has been undermined through rationalism and empiricism.
3. The Word of God has been proclaimed in a cold, abrasive, and judgmental manner.
4. Insensitive and overaggressive personal evangelism.
5. Unhappy experiences in church-related small groups.
6. Culturally irrelevant worship services.
7. Too frequent changes of minister.
8. No effective procedures for incorporating newcomers.
9. Unresolved personal conflicts.
10. Institutional degeneration.[14]

One or more of these deficiencies drove the majority of Armstrong's early converts into his arms. The Armstrong alternative to nominalism, however, had little substance. It provided little more than a substitution of legalistic Sabbatarianism and prophetic emotionalism for sound, Christ-centered proclamation of the gospel.

Herbert Armstrong was a powerful and dynamic preacher who was excellent at pointing out certain deficiencies in other Christian churches. In Armstrong's church, though, the Bible became a tool to "prove" that Armstrong was God's man with God's message and God's "restored truth" and that Armstrong's group was God's one and only true church. The gospel of the kingdom of God was spiritually gutted, becoming principally an announcement about a future millennial reign of Christ over the physical nations and in practice a message of obedience to the law—especially the Sabbath, the annual holy days, and God's government through Herbert Armstrong.

The true gospel, on the other hand, calls sinful humans to salvation by God's grace through faith in Christ. That salvation is not empty, to be sure, but it entails *repentance* accompanied by a *life of discipleship*. "Take up your cross and follow me," Jesus commands. Armstrong's attempt to resolve the nominality problem consistently fails on this fundamental truth of Scripture: Jesus calls *sinners* to himself, not people who have already turned from sin (cf. Mark 2:17). Humans are by nature sinners. They cannot loose themselves from the bondage of sin. They can only cry out, as did the tax collector in Jesus' parable, "Lord, be merciful to me, a sinner!" It was this man, the acknowledged sinner, not the "obedient" Pharisee, who went away justified, says Jesus.

Regarding Christians who believe in God's existence but do not know God in personal experience, A. W. Tozer observed, "They go through life trying to love an ideal and be loyal to a mere principle."[15] In the Worldwide Church of God, the ideal was to belong to the right church organization, the one that fit our ideal conception; and the principle was the "way of life," especially Sabbath keeping and loyalty to Armstrong, which we believed to be virtuous. But God calls his people into community with *him*, the divine *Person*, to a true and real relationship, not to a mere divine *principle*, code of conduct, or set of ideal behaviors. Armstrong's concept of the "true church" was a church that had "all the right doctrines" as he understood them. With such a concept as the basis for relationship with God, it is no wonder that WCG members tended to measure human standing with God by a person's level of successful adherence to the selected set of "right doctrines."

AGING APOSTLE

As Herbert Armstrong aged, and especially after some heart trouble in 1977, his physical ability to lead the church became more and more questionable. Decisions of any significance could not be made without his approval, yet getting to him became difficult if not impossible. Church officials often feared making decisions of any consequence, knowing that Armstrong might disapprove and reverse them. It was not uncommon for the aging Armstrong to grant approval for a project to one official, only to tell another to stop it. Sometimes he would forget that he had approved a given proposal and dress down the "presumptuous" official in front of others.

This situation naturally bred jealousy and infighting among officials close to Armstrong as he privately confided his distrust or dissatisfaction with one to another, changing his confidants and enemies like clothing. He seemed to trust no one completely, fearing that this one or that one was trying to "take over" and expressing his worries "in confidence" to others. As one official put it, "At one time or another every evangelist [the highest ecclesiastical office in the Worldwide Church of God under Armstrong] has had Mr. Armstrong tell him that he doubts the conversion of another one."

Some days, the aging patriarch might be congenial and lucid, reviewing principles of effective writing with the editorial staff, discussing strategic plans for buying television time, or speaking to a training session for pastors. Other days, he might be in a rage over an anonymous letter, calling in employees one by one, pounding his desk, and demanding to know whether they wrote it or knew who did. His hearing was poor. His vision was gone in one eye and dim in the other. He had to use a strong magnifying glass to read. He feared that people close to him were conspiring against him—as, indeed, several had over the years.

During Armstrong's final years, the church was virtually at a standstill administratively. Most of his energy and time was consumed with personal issues—his relationship with his second wife and ensuing divorce, his son's "rebellion" and efforts to "take over the church," and his own failing health. There was little, if any, harmony between major church leaders and departments. Frustration and distrust were rampant at church headquarters in Pasadena. There was no coordinated strategic planning and no concept of preparing for the long-term integrity of the church organization. Every church leader had his own idea of "how Mr. Armstrong thinks" and what Mr. Armstrong "would do" in any given situation.

Even in the midst of administrative turmoil, WCG mission continued to center around one thing: warning the United States and other white, English-speaking countries to repent before the German-led European beast power rises and destroys them with nuclear weapons—the bombs are about to start falling—after which Christ will return and set up the kingdom (with WCG members as his glorified administrative team, of course). But without consistent and coordinated leadership, every church official had his own idea of how that "commission" ought to be carried out and what church priorities should be.

GOD'S MAN

Church officials did seem to agree on one thing: Herbert Armstrong was God's man, and whatever he decided to do was God's will. If a department head could get Armstrong's approval of his particular plan for "carrying out the commission," he could confidently disregard the ideas, needs, and priorities of other administrators. If he had (or thought he had) Armstrong's backing, then he had (or thought he had) God's backing. Armstrong seemed oblivious to the administrative nightmare his one-man-show style of leadership created. If there were problems, he reasoned, they were the fault of underlings; if there were successes, God was blessing Armstrong's leadership.

Until his final months, if it ever seriously entered the mind of Herbert Armstrong that the church he founded would have to endure for any significant period beyond his lifetime, he certainly never let on. His administrative policies were fundamentally geared to the premise that Christ would return before his death. When Armstrong occasionally mused on the idea of succession, it amounted to a list of reasons why every leading administrator was unsuited for the task.

Serious attention to succession might never have come up at all had Armstrong not learned in 1981 that certain church officials were allegedly arranging to have him declared mentally incompetent and have a legal conservator appointed for him. His response was to appoint what he termed the "Advisory Council of Elders," which was empowered to appoint a successor in the event of his death or during the duration of any incapacity to govern, unless he personally named a successor first. Even then the fundamental motivation was not to introduce sound principles of leadership but rather to circumvent an alleged plan to have a conservator appointed. Even at that point, Armstrong still believed he would not die before the return of Jesus.[16]

TKACH APPOINTED

WCG administrative structure was clear and ironclad: Armstrong could not be removed from office. When he appointed Joseph Tkach Sr. to succeed him as pastor general, Armstrong strongly charged Tkach to carefully safeguard this hierarchical structure that kept final authority solely in the hands of the pastor general.

"If you allow them to put your decisions into the hands of a board, this will no longer be the government of God. It would be the government of men," Armstrong told Tkach. "God has always worked through one man to lead his church." Tkach did not change the structure, though he voluntarily sought a wide range of input before implementing major decisions. He was reluctant to act without general consensus among his leadership team and rarely did so. Ironically, however, *Tkach would not have been able to implement the massive doctrinal transformation that characterized the later years of his administration without the unfettered hierarchical authority delegated to him by Armstrong.* For Tkach, reaching consensus among top-ranking ministers became increasingly difficult as each domino of doctrinal and administrative revision fell.

Upon his death in September 1995, Tkach delegated the same unchecked authority to his son, Joseph Tkach Jr., making him the third pastor general of the church. The younger Tkach immediately adopted, voluntarily, a consensual style of leadership and began to act only with approval from the church board of directors. He began the process of reviewing and revising church bylaws in early 1996. This was made easier by the fact that rigid doctrinal opposition in the administration no longer existed.

It is a fact of history that absolute authority is dangerous in the hands of any human. For a church to be spiritually healthy, its leader must submit to accountability within a group of faithful Christians and must be subject to removal under certain circumstances. It is true that the same hierarchical authority that allowed the Worldwide Church of God to become what it had been was also necessary for it to change. For the church to continue on a spiritually healthy path, however, the authoritarian form of church government will have to be appropriately modified. I am happy to say that the process of doing so is well underway.

Under the leadership of Joseph Tkach Sr., the Worldwide Church of God began the painful and traumatic process of major doctrinal and institutional change.

Herbert W. Armstrong and his wife, Loma, with their first two children, Beverly and Dorothy, about 1922.

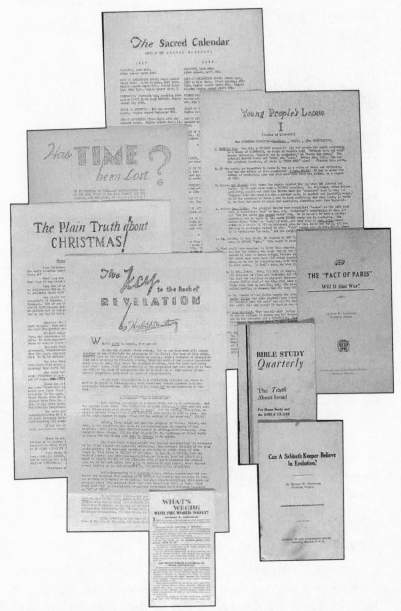

Some of Herbert W. Armstrong's early articles and brochures published by the Church of God, a small sabbatarian denomination headquartered in Stanberry, Missouri.

LIGHT SHINES IN
MY DARKNESS

IN EARLY 1991 MY grandmother was close to the end of her life, and she knew it. I had flown to Amarillo, Texas, joining other family members to celebrate her eighty-fifth birthday. As she and I sat talking in the small room of her convalescent home, I could see she had something on her mind. She put her hand on mine, looked into my eyes, and asked slowly, in her stroke-slurred speech, "Mick—[she always called me "Mick"]—do you love Jesus?"

I am chagrined to say that I was uncomfortable with the question. We just didn't talk like that in the Worldwide Church of God. That was Protestant talk. Syrupy sweet. We wanted to be asked, "Do you *obey* Jesus *Christ?*" We didn't like to say "Jesus" without adding "Christ." That sounded manlier, more powerful to us. Just saying "Jesus" sounded wimpy and sickly sweet. And now here was my stroke-stricken grandmother, whom I would not want to hurt or disappoint for the world, asking me if I loved Jesus. I could hardly get the words out, but thank God I said, "Yes, I love Jesus, Grandma."

"Oh, I'm so glad," she said.

Looking back on it, it seems strange. I considered myself a Christian, but I had trouble saying "I love Jesus." I would die for Jesus, I thought, but don't ask me to say the words "I love Jesus." What kind of Christian experience teaches people to think like that?

The simple fact was, I *didn't* love Jesus the way Jesus would yet teach me to love him. I loved him in a human, carnal sort of way—my way. I loved him as an extension of me: he was my champion, my hero, my king. But he was not yet my friend. I knew a lot *about* him. But I didn't yet know *him*.

What I am saying is that as long as the heir is a child, he is no different from a slave, although he owns the whole estate. He is subject to guardians and trustees until the time set by his father. So also, when we were children, we were in slavery under the basic principles of the world. But when the time had fully come, God sent his Son, born of a woman, born under law, to redeem those under law, that we might receive the full rights of sons. Because you are sons, God sent the Spirit of his Son into our hearts, the Spirit who calls out, "*Abba*, Father." So you are no longer a slave, but a son; and since you are a son, God has made you also an heir. (Gal. 4:1–7)

I had been a slave in the household of God. Not because I had to be a slave, but because I didn't yet realize what it meant that God had made me his child. I lived like a slave because that was all I knew. I followed the rules I thought were the Master's rules because I honored the Master and because I wanted to avoid the lash and receive the benefits.

It was a better life than people outside the household had to live. It kept me out of a lot of trouble. But at best it was only a shell of the true life God yearned for me to have. God wanted a *son*, not a slave. God wanted a relationship of *love*, not a relationship of rules. God wanted my *heart and soul*, not just my compliance.

Belonging to the "one and only" is heady stuff. You are special. You know things nobody else knows. You do things the deceived masses do not do, and you avoid things the deceived masses embrace. Your human leader is the most important person on earth. Because of your special status, you will be delivered from the disasters that are coming on the world. All the people that oppose you now will one day acknowledge that you were right all along and praise you for your faithfulness and integrity—that is, if they finally join the "one and only" and escape annihilation. But the light of God's love was about to break into the darkness of my "loyalty and integrity."

ARMSTRONG AND PHYSICAL HEALING

Herbert Armstrong had taught anointing with oil and prayer for physical healing from the beginning of his ministry. In his autobiography, he described his first encounter with God's power to heal when his wife, Loma, contracted blood poisoning:

> This man actually dared to talk directly to God, and to tell God what He had promised to do! He quoted the promises of God to heal. He applied them to my wife. He literally held God to what He had promised! It was not because we, as mortal humans, deserved what he asked, but through the merits of Jesus Christ, and according to God's great mercy.
>
> He merely claimed God's PROMISE to heal. He asked God to heal her completely, from the top of her head to the bottom of her feet.
>
> "You have promised," he said to God, "and you have given us the right to hold you to your promise to heal by the power of your mighty Holy Spirit. I hold you to that promise! We expect to have the answer!"
>
> Never have I heard anyone talk like that to God!
>
> It was not a long prayer—perhaps a minute or two. But as he spoke I knew that as sure as there is a God in heaven, my wife had to be healed! Any other result would have made God out a liar. Any other result would have nullified the authority of the Scriptures. Complete assurance seized me—and also my wife. We simply knew that she was

released from everything that had gripped her—she was freed from the sickness—she was healed! To have doubted would have been to doubt God—to doubt the Bible. It simply never occurred to us to doubt. We believed! We knew![1]

Armstrong goes on to recount how Loma woke up the next morning completely healed of everything, "including some long-standing internal maladjustments" (319). His conclusion? "The Bible is filled with thousands of God's promises. They are there for us to claim."

The result of this woeful misunderstanding of God's freedom to act according to his own perfect will, in accordance with his love, and in the best interests of his people was disastrous. Members who were not healed were looked upon as weak in faith or as guilty of some hidden sin. People who "died in the faith" because they refused traditional medical treatment were considered automatically saved, not because Jesus' righteousness was attributed to them, but because they "obeyed God to the end," trusting him and not drugs and surgery for healing.

To submit to drugs and surgery (except for first aid and what Armstrong called "repair surgery") was a sin of the highest order, not only a lack of faith in God for healing, but in essence a bowing down before the altar of Baal. There was no middle ground. It was either/or. You could not take drugs or have surgery *and* trust God for healing. Even vaccination was considered sinful. Most WCG parents sent notes to school with their children requesting they be excused on religious grounds from mandatory vaccinations. An article in the church magazine of 1961 made the church position crystal clear:

> There are numerous scriptures in the Bible which point out to us that we are to rely, not on man, but on God for our healing (see Psa.103:3). When we put our faith in men and their drugs and vaccines, rather than in God who has ALL POWER, we are actually putting man and his ingenuity before the Creator God. If we are to

rely on God's healing power, it is impossible to rely also on medicines and vaccines developed by men.

Those in the Church of God follow the instruction given by the Apostle James (James 5:14–16) and rely on God's healing power through prayer for the healing of sickness and disease. As believers in God's healing power and DIVINE PROTECTION, true Christians cannot put their faith in the methods of men by submitting them-selves to drugs and vaccines.

Your faith is either in Almighty God, the only true Healer and Protector, or in the god of medicine (II Kings 1:1–4), drugs and vaccines. Where is your faith and who is your God?[2]

Naturally, members who chose traditional medicine for themselves or their children usually did so in secret, and they usually carried the pain of secret guilt. By the time Armstrong died in January 1986, the stigma had lifted somewhat. Still, members who used traditional medicine were considered weak in faith, and many pastors still refused to anoint and pray for them, since they had chosen Baal over God for their healing.

CRISIS OF FAITH

It was in that context that I found myself with a very sick child in the winter of 1986. Our five-year-old son Jeff had been ill for more than a week with a recurring high fever. He would be up and around for a while, then he would lie down on the floor with a high fever. My wife, Victoria, tried to keep liquids in him and keep him in bed, and then he would feel better and want to get up and play. But before long, he would be down again. All the while, he had a little nagging cough.

I anointed him and prayed for him and trusted God to heal him. I think we may have had other ministers come and pray for him as well. But he didn't improve, and we became more and more worried.

We got some books about childhood illnesses and symptoms and what to do about them. We found that Jeff's symptoms indicated that he had pneumonia. Needless to say, we were in a panic. Our son was in danger of dying. He was clearly becoming dehydrated, and his fever was no longer going away.

What should we do? Should we continue to trust God to heal him, or should we "weaken" and take him to the doctor? The books told us that antibiotics would cure our son. But antibiotics were a product of Satan's pharmaceutical deception, weren't they? To take antibiotics would be like going to Satan for help and telling God we didn't trust him, wouldn't it?

I began praying for God to help me understand all this. Was he calling me to give up my son, like Abraham was asked to do? To go to the doctor and take the antibiotics would be so simple and seemed so sensible. But surely that was Satan's deception, trying to get me to abandon faith in God and go over to the "dark side."

We got out the Bible and our church literature on healing. We studied the church teaching and all the Bible references it cited. And we continued to pray for God to help us make sense of all this. Meanwhile, Jeff simply lay there with his now slightly sunken five-year-old eyes looking up at the parents whom God had charged with his care and nurture.

THE LIGHT SHINES IN MY DARKNESS

As I continued to cry out in prayer, my assumptions about divine healing being incompatible with medical science began to melt away. It began to occur to me that God expects parents to take proper care of their children. It began to occur to me that proper care includes taking appropriate medicines. I began to realize that binding wounds and setting bones is not fundamentally different from necessary surgery and taking medicine. And I couldn't get past the plain fact that Luke, author of one of the

Gospels, *is plainly called a physician in the Bible!* Furthermore, nowhere does the Bible even suggest that getting medical attention is wrong. Every passage cited in our literature as proof that "going to the doctors" was a sin was taken out of context, misapplied, and misinterpreted.

Yes, God heals. But God protects too. Does that mean we should never call the police? God provides our needs. Does that mean we shouldn't get a job or save money? The fact that God heals does not mean we shouldn't bind wounds, use medicine, and take sensible care of ourselves.

Suddenly I understood that I had no right to withhold antibiotics from my child. Even if I wanted to make such a choice for myself, I had no right to impose that choice on my minor child. If he had a choice, would he choose to refuse medicine and die of pneumonia? Or was I making that choice for him? Was Abraham's situation normative for me—or for *any* Christian, for that matter? Had God spoken to me as he did to Abraham? Had God told me to go and sacrifice my son? And was withholding normal medical attention the same as Abraham's being told directly by God to go to Mount Moriah and make a sacrifice (which God in fact *stopped* him from making, of course)?

No! God does *not* condemn medical science. He does *not* expect parents to withhold modern medicine from their children. He does *not* forbid Christians to become doctors nurses, or pharmacologists. Keeping Jeff from antibiotics was just plain *wrong*, and all my ideas about God's healing and medical science being opposites were just plain *wrong*.

We got an Ambassador College student to babysit our daughter, Elizabeth. We bundled up Jeff, put him in his car seat, and took him to the emergency room. The doctor gave him a chest x-ray, confirmed a serious case of pneumonia, gave him a shot of penicillin, and prescribed a course of antibiotics. Within twenty-four hours our son was nearly back to normal. Had we not gone to the doctor when we did, Jeff might have died within days. And I suppose Victoria and I would have been considered by our church to be faithful servants of God who were willing even to give up our son for the Lord. And even worse, maybe we would have agreed.

Praise God for his grace!

I have to say that even though I could plainly see that what Victoria and I had done was right and was what God wanted us to do, I still felt pangs of guilt and doubt. Old habits and beliefs die hard. Even when the intellect accepts new truth, the heart sometimes lags behind.

I found myself afraid to tell other members about our trip to the emergency room and our use of antibiotics. I feared we would be condemned. But I did feel I could discuss it with Joseph Tkach Sr.

THE TEACHING CHANGES

Over the next several days, I explained to Mr. Tkach what I had discovered in studying our literature and comparing it with the Bible. He was quite interested and told me that he had been thinking along similar lines. He asked me to write up the study, and he began to discuss the subject with other church leaders. He found a fairly positive response from most.

Kyriakos Stavrinides, an Ambassador College faculty member, was a friend and frequent research resource for Tkach. Stavrinides explained to Tkach that Armstrong's idea of the sacrifice of Christ being segmented into shed blood for "spiritual sin" and broken body for "physical sin" was erroneous. Instead, Jesus' sacrifice was one unified whole for the whole redemption of humanity.

Armstrong had believed that Jesus' body was broken specifically and solely that we might be physically healed. Our spiritual redemption came through Jesus' shed blood, Armstrong taught. It was on this basis that Armstrong took such a strong stand against modern medical science. After all, if the only reason Jesus was beaten with a cat-o-nine-tails was so that our "physical sins" might be forgiven and our bodies healed, then how dare we set that aside in favor of drugs and surgery?

The acid test, however, was always *Plain Truth* editor Herman Hoeh, one of the founding students of Ambassador College and one of longest-serving ordained ministers in the church. Tkach really did not expect Hoeh to counter Armstrong's teaching. But Hoeh expressed his support and told a surprised Tkach that he had personally disagreed with Armstrong on this point from the earliest days of the college. Hoeh even gave Tkach a tract he had kept since his college days that countered the idea that using medical science is a sin.

Hoeh's positive response provided Tkach with the emotional support he needed to ask me to begin drafting an article to all ministers and members announcing a change in the church's teaching on the use of medical science. We published the article in March of 1987 in the *Pastor General's Report* for all ministers worldwide. *The Worldwide News*, the official member publication, presented the article to all members a few weeks later.

Little did we realize it at the time, but this change was virtually insignificant compared to what would soon follow. It was only a matter of months before it began to be clear that there were also major problems with Armstrong's doctrinal linchpin—his approach to end-time prophecy and his teaching on British Israelism.

CHRISTMAS AND MR. ROGERS

Although I didn't see it that way at the time, the first faint stirrings of cognitive dissonance that Victoria and I had about the Worldwide Church of God happened a couple of years earlier when our two oldest children, Jeff and Liz, were about four and three years old, respectively. We had just finished breakfast one weekday morning, and the four of us were watching *Mr.*

Rogers' Neighborhood on TV before I left for work, part of our regular morning routine in those days.

Mr. Rogers is a good man who speaks in a kindly, gentle way to his small viewers as he teaches them about everything from factories to fire trucks and from goldfish to cookie making. He also teaches them about the difference between reality and make-believe, even while he uses make-believe to illustrate moral lessons. We were grateful for such a valuable program and such a positive adult role model.

Our children respected Mr. Rogers and trusted him. On this morning, however, Mr. Rogers caught us by surprise. He opened a package containing a Santa Claus costume, complete with beard. Slowly and gently he explained and demonstrated to the children how the beard fits on the face but that the same person is still under it. It was a great segment. But it was about Santa Claus—and Santa Claus is bad. But Mr. Rogers is good. But Santa Claus is bad. But Mr. Rogers is good.

"Dad."

I felt it coming miles away.

"Dad," Liz repeated, her little furrowed brow staring at the TV. "Dad, why is Mr. Rogers putting on Santa Claus clothes? Is Mr. Rogers bad?"

"I want to know too, Dad. Is Mr. Rogers bad?" Jeff echoed, not moving his wide eyes from the shocking drama unfolding on the TV.

"No." I stammered for the right words. "No. Mr. Rogers isn't bad. He, uh, just doesn't, uh, know that Santa Claus is bad. He, uh, uh, is just trying to help people not be scared of Santa Claus."

"But he's dressing up like Santa Claus, Dad. Is Santa Claus good?" Jeff pointed at the TV screen.

"Well, no. Santa Claus isn't good. It's just that Mr. Rogers doesn't know that Santa Claus is bad. Someday he'll know, and then he won't dress up like Santa Claus anymore."

They just stared at the screen and didn't talk any more. Victoria and I did too. And the gears started turning. "Out of the mouths of babes," the proverb says, "shall come wisdom." And it had that day. It began to dawn on us that we had no problem letting the kids have their pictures taken with Mickey Mouse and Goofy. But this kind old gentleman who brings gifts to children on Christmas Eve was bad, bad, bad. Why?

Well, it is not because of gifts, per se. Gifts are not a sin. It is not because there is no literal Santa Claus, and he is only a story. Stories are not sin; the parables of Jesus, for example, were stories. It is not because of red clothes or snow or reindeer. Red clothes, snow, and reindeer are not sins. It is not because of the white beard. White beards are not sin. So what is it, then? It has to be because he does it on Christmas, I guess. And Christmas is definitely bad. So Santa Claus must be bad too, because he is associated with Christmas.

PAGAN ORIGINS

Christians who condemn Christmas have their reasons. Prior to the fourth century, December 25 *was indeed* a day of pagan merrymaking in the Roman Empire in honor of the birthday of the "invincible sun." It marked the lengthening of days following the winter solstice. The dying sun, indicated by the shorter days of winter, was "reborn" at this time and began to increase again in strength, as shown by the longer days. How can a day devoted to pagan revelry be used to honor Christ? Furthermore, there is no biblical precedent for birthday celebrations. Did not only such people as Pharaoh and Herod hold celebrations on their birthdays? The early church father Origen, for example, condemned the concept of celebrating Jesus' birth at all.

Perhaps these are good reasons for Christians to avoid any celebration of Christmas. People should certainly not violate their consciences. I know many devoted and faithful Christian hearts who love Jesus tenderly yet avoid Christmas for such reasons of conscience.

To the contrary, perhaps December 25 was ultimately settled on by Christians for celebrating the birth of Christ precisely so that the Christian observance would coincide with the pagan festival—so as to overshadow and replace it—which, of course, it did. Jesus Christ was worshiped as the *true* Light of the world (John 1:9) and the *true* Sun of righteousness who rises with healing in his wings (Mal. 4:2).

CONSCIENCE AND CONDEMNATION

The Christmas tree is highly offensive to some Christians, who consider it a leftover from pagan revelry and nature worship.[3] It is interesting, however, that Yahweh is not reluctant to compare himself to a pine tree. In Hosea 14:8, Yahweh pleads:

> O Ephraim, what more have I to do with idols?
> > I will answer him and care for him.
> I am like a green pine tree;
> > your fruitfulness comes from me.

Thus, in direct contrast to idols, God compares himself to a green pine tree as a symbol that he is the only source of the fruitfulness of his people.

I know of no Christians who *worship* the Christmas tree. Perhaps there are some, but I have never heard of them. While I respect and understand the viewpoint and decision of Christians who avoid Christmas, I have come to view it in a fresh way—a way that provides another excellent opportunity to focus and orient my life around the saving and empowering work of God through Jesus Christ. I wrote the following short description of how I now understand the Christmas tree for my *One Pilgrim's Progress* column in the *Plain Truth* magazine:

THE CHRISTIAN CHRISTMAS TREE

The evergreen tree symbolizes the faithfulness of God,
remaining forever the same,
even during the darkness and cold of winter.

The candles (or lights) on the tree symbolize our Savior Jesus Christ,
whose life was the Light of all people,
the Light that shines in the darkness,
and which enlightens everyone.

Some people put red bows on the tree,
symbolizing the shed blood of our Savior,
by which our sins are forgiven.

Ornaments symbolize fruit,
which in turn symbolizes the gracious gifts and provision
of God for his people.

Just as the Cross of Christ
was a tree stripped of its greenery and dignity
and made into a dead post,
so our sin has stripped us of beauty and dignity
and resulted in death.

Through the death of the Son of God on the dead tree,
and by his resurrection and life,
salvation and true life have come to the whole creation,
especially to us,
whose dignity and value and beauty has been restored
through faith in him.

The splendor of the Christmas tree,
decorated with light and color and beauty,
symbolizes our restored and reconciled state by the grace of God.

Our Father in heaven and our Lord Jesus Christ love us,
and have made us beautiful
by the good things they have done for us.

The gifts under the tree
symbolize the dignity and value God has given to human beings
through Jesus' saving work.

We give gifts to one another on this day for one reason only:
God sent his Son into the world to save us
and make us his children,
and has placed his love into us,
that we might love one another, even as he loves us.

That's what Christmas is about—the love of God.
And that's the story the Christmas tree tells us on this Christ-
    mas season.

There is no sin in approaching these matters differently. The Bible is silent about the celebration of Christmas. There was no sin in the Worldwide Church of God's avoiding Christmas for reasons of conscience. The sin lay in our unrelenting condemnation of all Christians who viewed the matter differently from the way we did. If we had followed Paul's admonition in Romans 14 in regard to matters of days devoted to the Lord, we could have lived by our preference without turning it into an occasion to condemn others.

Our younger son, Christopher, has grown up with Christmas and Easter. Each year at Easter time, I love to ask him what rabbits and eggs have to do with Jesus' resurrection. "They are symbols of new life," he eagerly responds. "Symbols of the new life we have in Jesus!" As Dr. Watson used to say to Sherlock Holmes, "How absurdly simple."

SUPPORTING THE MYTH

Being the only true church is heady wine. It feels very good to be God's chosen few, the faithful remnant. And controversial issues like pagan influences on Christmas and Easter, ironically, provide just the needed rationale to help support the myth that your group constitutes the loyal and obedient faithful few. It is another way of drawing a boundary around the grace of God. It is another way of declaring: "God's grace reaches to us and no farther. How is that so? Because we are the faithful ones. We are the ones who have not been deluded. We are not like the deceived majority. Satan has deceived the whole world, but he has not deceived us, because we are the elect. And here's more proof: Christmas and Easter are pagan, and we don't keep them."

Condemning others is a fine way of making ourselves feel less condemned. *At least* I don't keep a pagan holiday. *At least* I keep the Sabbath. *At least* I don't smoke. Or as one very proper church lady said, as she turned up her nose at a frightened, confused, and depressed pregnant teenager who got up enough courage to attend a church service, "*At least* I haven't committed *that* sin."

Loving Jesus

The grace of God does not have boundaries. We have boundaries, but God does not. We have our rules, our ways of measuring others to keep them out. God invites them in. We are so "holy and pure" that we are judgmental. God is full of grace and mercy. We know the "truth." God *is* the Truth.

I am so grateful that God is not like me or like anybody else. I am so grateful that he does not draw boundaries that leave people out on account of what they do. He is the prodigal Father—prodigal in his grace. He is the ever watchful, lovesick Parent, who will receive even the most wayward with outstretched arms, running at full pace to meet them and put shoes on their feet and his ring on their finger. He receives me, and he receives all who turn toward him.

Our petty ideas about pagan origins and outward appearances evaporate under the intense heat of God's love. God is not interested in our self-aggrandizing quarrels about theological details. He is interested in *us*.

> For God so loved the world that he gave his one and only Son, that whoever believes in him shall not perish but have eternal life. (John 3:16)

Our theological disputes seem bent on *separating* us from each other. God is bent on bringing us together in Christ. Is theology important? Yes, it is even crucial—when it is about who God is and what he has done to save the world. That is just the point. Jesus came to save sinners, of whom I am chief. I don't need hair-splitting definitions of sin. I need Jesus Christ, my Savior, Lord, and Teacher.

Praise God for Fred Rogers and Santa Claus! Praise God for the Easter Bunny and chocolate eggs! *Today in the town of David a Savior has been born to you. He is Christ, the Lord.* I celebrate on Christmas and Easter because by the grace of God, and only by the grace of God, I love Jesus.

Herbert W. Armstrong in an early World Tomorrow *television broadcast.*

A Bible class at Ambassador College in Big Sandy, Texas.

Mayfair, acquired by Ambassador College in 1949, to become the first student residence on the Pasadena campus. The bargain purchase of the neglected Mayfair property doubled the size of the fledgling campus.

"THE ONLY TRUE CHURCH"

IT MAY COME AS some surprise to those outside the Worldwide Church of God when I say that the greatest error of the Worldwide Church of God was not in the fact that it held distinctive doctrinal positions. There is no significant danger in a church retaining distinctives that are *not destructive to fellowship and unity in the body of Christ* (cf. Rom. 14). But distinctives must not be allowed to take center stage in proclamation or in practice. If they do, community and unity will invariably be the casualty. Distinctives must remain peripheral and background, and in no way should they be tests of fellowship.

In the Worldwide Church of God, however, church distinctives became the message, the identity, the reason for being, and the justification for the condemnation of all of historic Christianity and all Christian churches. As tests of fellowship, they rose to a level equal to that of the gospel itself and in fact crowded the gospel into the dark corners of the stage.

There is no question that Armstrong's commitment to Scripture was admirable. His commitment to a devoted life based on the principles, teachings, and disciplines of the Bible was also admirable. But Armstrong's idea that obedience to a specified set of criteria designated his church as the only true and faithful body of Christians on earth led to a church membership devoted to careful obedience of biblical law yet characterized by pride, fear, manipulation, and a judgmental spirit.

Armstrong believed that God would save only those people who eventually came to be members of his church.[1] The resulting spiritual pride was equaled only by his fear of losing control. His condemnation of any and all who questioned his absolute authority was swift and powerful. A group of leaders Armstrong disfellowshiped in 1974 for an "attempted coup" were branded as "liberals," "liars," "covetous," "selfish," "political conspirers," and "revolutionaries"—not to mention "thieves," "malcontents," "embittered, angered, revenge-seeking disfellowshiped former members," "disgruntled troublemakers," "contentious, accusing, bickering troublemakers" and "embittered self-seeking men."[2] And all this in only six paragraphs!

Kenneth Stokes encourages members of any faith community to embrace questioning and doubt as part of a healthy pathway toward maturity in faith. Far from promoting a "believe whatever you like" or a "do whatever you like" approach to faith, Stokes observes that "the truly vital community of faith will help its people explore the options and possibilities, and discover for themselves those answers to their questions that will help them find the fullest possible personal faith for their lives."[3] Stokes encourages churches to affirm the searching hearts of their members: "'I'm glad you are asking those questions. They are important. Let's explore them together.'"[4] In Armstrong's church, by contrast, questions that even appeared to pose a challenge to Armstrong's exclusive right to religious control were simply not tolerated.

Herbert Armstrong's church spent as much, if not more, sermon time, ink, and airtime defending its unique doctrines and affirming its spiritual rightness over against all other "professing" Christian churches as it did proclaiming the gospel. The goal of Armstrong's Worldwide Church of God proclamation could be described as threefold:

1. Sounding an alarm, or "warning witness," about the sins, deficiencies, errors, and shortcomings of rival groups—in this case, all other Christian churches as well as society at large.

2. Announcing that Jesus Christ will return to earth to destroy the wicked, reward the faithful (meaning Herbert Armstrong and loyal WCG members, as well as all Sabbath-keeping saints prior to Armstrong) and set up the kingdom of God on the physical earth.

3. Bringing new converts into "the church"—in this case, into the Worldwide Church of God, or more precisely, into the teachings of Herbert Armstrong.

Group distinctives, not the biblical Christian gospel, became the reason to align oneself with the group. The rationale usually went something like this:

1. Only we have the "true" gospel of the future kingdom of God.

2. Only we keep all the commandments of God, including the Sabbath and the annual holy days.

3. Only we are truly warning the world about the coming punishments on the modern descendants of the lost tribes of Israel.

4. Only we have the biblical form of church government, which is from the top down.

5. Only we truly love and obey God with all our hearts, especially through keeping the Sabbath, which is the "test commandment," making us the true faithful remnant.

6. Therefore, you must join us or be severely punished by the wrath of God.

The concept of simply proclaiming the grace and power of God in Jesus Christ and letting the Holy Spirit lead the hearers into whatever fellowship he wills was hopelessly buried under the stipulations of "right doctrine" and "right obedience" as deciphered by Armstrong, the "only true end-time apostle of God." The result for most members was what Paul called "having a form of godliness but denying its power" (2 Tim. 3:5).

IDENTITY IN THE SABBATH, NOT IN JESUS

Andrew Murray described the Christian life as "no longer a vain struggle to live *right*, but a resting in Christ to find strength in Him *as* life. He helps us fight and gain the victory of faith!"[5] The Worldwide Church of God found its spiritual identity primarily in the weekly Sabbath, missing out on the power and joy of spiritual rest in Jesus Christ.

Because it was not being bathed in the gospel and because it believed its own members to be the only real Christians, the Worldwide Church of God was incapable of discerning the work and presence of the Holy Spirit in the lives of people outside its own walls. The work of the Spirit in other Christians was often minimized in sermons with such derogatory references as "self-righteous," "insincere," and "goody-good vanity." The definition of *Christian* was skewed in the Worldwide Church of God. A Christian was one in whom the Holy Spirit dwelled—a good definition on the surface. The catch was that the Spirit only dwelled in members of the Worldwide Church of God.

With such an inward, exclusivist mindset as that promoted by the Worldwide Church of God, a person is incapable of freely and joyously obeying Jesus' command to love one another (John 13:35). It is not possible to love another disciple *as a fellow disciple* when you are calling him a child of the devil. You can *say* that you actually love all people, even those who are deceived, but such a declaration rings absurdly hollow in the presence of Jesus' undiluted command to his disciples. This, I believe, was the fundamental sin of the Worldwide Church of God: it condemned the witness and work of the Spirit in everyone who was not of the "right tradition," did not hold the "right set of doctrines," and did not obey the "right set of laws."

The WCG Sabbath doctrine tended to shield us from the penetration of the Spirit into the deepest and darkest corners of our hearts precisely because our Sabbath keeping deceived us into believing we had already achieved the most vital aspect of right standing with God—observing his Sabbath day. We loved the law, and we thought we loved Jesus; but ironically, our sense of law keeping led us to condemn Jesus' brothers and sisters. Andrew Murray said it well: "My relationship with God is part of my relationship with men. Failure in one will cause failure in the other."[6]

Doctrinal statements can be restudied and rewritten. Hearts, on the other hand, must be broken before they can be changed. Poor doctrine can sometimes be a matter of mere ignorance, lack of education, poor exegetical skills, weak communications skills, or plain misunderstanding or misinterpretation. But hearts that are arrogant, self-serving, smug, or self-righteous must die and be reborn. A man can have a pure heart before God and yet hold any number of "wrong" doctrines. But he can also articulate every doctrine precisely "according to Hoyle" and yet have an unregenerate heart of stone. Thomas à Kempis wrote:

> What good does it do, then, to debate about the Trinity, if by lack of humility you are displeasing to the Trinity? In truth, lofty words do not make a person holy and just, but a virtuous life makes one dear to God. I would much rather feel profound sorrow for my sins than be able to define the theological term for it. If you knew the whole Bible by heart and the sayings of all the philosophers, what good would it all be without God's love and grace?[7]

"BY THIS SHALL EVERYONE KNOW"

How ironic that on one hand, the Worldwide Church of God called for faithful obedience to all the commandments of God, even seeing itself in Revelation 12:17 as the faithful remnant who "obey God's commandments and hold to the testimony of Jesus"; yet on the other hand, it failed monumentally in the one commandment Jesus gave as the "sign" by which people would know who are his disciples—"that you love one another."

The doctrinal distinctives of the Worldwide Church of God led it not into Jesus' love, but into a spirit of distrust and condemnation of fellow Christians. The Worldwide Church of God confused biblical discipleship with group discipleship. The sentiment was more one of "Follow us" than it was one of "Follow Christ." In fact, Armstrong led members to tend to see these as the same thing. To follow Herbert Armstrong was to follow Jesus Christ, since Armstrong was "Christ's man." And anyone who didn't follow Herbert Armstrong, or worse, who opposed his teachings, was an enemy of Christ.[8]

It is significant that the way doctrinal questions were most often phrased by WCG members was "What do *we* say about . . . ?" There was no encouragement for members to think for themselves or to search out answers to questions through research or reflection. All research was to be done in WCG publications, and virtually all non-WCG Christian literature was vilified. No member must be heard disagreeing with headquarters or with the local pastor. The WCG sense of identity was firmly in belonging to the group and believing what the group believed, for only in faithfulness to the group and its leader, Herbert Armstrong, would one be accounted worthy to escape the horrors of the coming tribulation.

HOLDING UP THE APOSTLE'S HANDS

Herbert Armstrong taught the members of his church that without his specially revealed, unique teachings and without loyalty toward, and support of, his personal ministry, they could not attain salvation. Armstrong viewed the members of his church as having been called primarily to back up and support him, God's apostle, through their "prayers, encouragement, tithes and offerings" in his call to proclaim the gospel to all the world.[9] He was God's only true apostle on earth today, he preached to his followers, and they were called now, not primarily for their own salvation, but rather to hold up his hands in the commission God had given him.

To Herbert Armstrong, the fundamental purpose of personal spiritual disciplines for Christians was twofold: (1) to support him in his special call of God, and (2) to qualify them to rule in the future kingdom of God. Armstrong put it this way:

> We have seen that Christ gave the lay body of the Church the SPECIAL MISSION to *back up* His apostles in their GOING FORTH with the Gospel to the world—with their prayers, encouragement, tithes and offerings.
>
> But this GIVING of their prayers, encouragement and financial support was GOD'S ASSIGNMENT *as the very means* of developing in *them* God's holy, righteous CHARACTER—that they, with the apostles and evangelists, may qualify to RULE with and under Christ in God's Kingdom. This *very means* of character development within the laity is THE WAY OF *GIVING*—not Satan's way of GETTING.[10]

It all boiled down to this simple formula: Herbert Armstrong (God's one and only true apostle and successor to the original twelve apostles), his work, and his teaching were church members' key to the kingdom. Do their part to believe his teachings and to support him, or miss out on what is needed to qualify to enter the kingdom of God.

MISPLACED ALLEGIANCE

I am struck by the plain truth in Frank Laubach's insightful statement: "The most subtle of all forms of selfishness is over-anxiety for ourselves to be more perfect than other people; not desiring that our neighbor shall be as perfect as we are."[11] A heart that loves cannot be a heart that thinks more highly of itself than of its neighbor. But that is precisely what we promoted in the Worldwide Church of God. We considered people who thought they belonged to Jesus but did not observe the Sabbath as we did to be deceived and not of Christ.

Thomas à Kempis observed: "If you want to learn something that will really help you, learn to see yourself as God sees you and not as you see yourself in the distorted mirror of your own self-importance."[12] That lovely teaching alone is enough to bring down the entire façade of Armstrongism.

Armstrongism is based on knowledge of, and allegiance to, Herbert Armstrong's teachings as the criteria for being the faithful people of God. It sets followers of Armstrong in a special category of acceptance by God apart from all other "professing" Christians. But people who truly see themselves as God sees them know that there is none righteous in the sight of God and that we all stand in God's presence only by his grace and only for the sake of his Son, Jesus Christ.

In biblical Christianity the playing field is level. We cannot progress in our new life in Christ until we understand that. Jesus won't force himself on us. He simply stands at the door and knocks. Only when we give up our personal or corporate "specialness" and recognize our desperate need for him who knocks, when we surrender unconditionally to the King and begin to place our broken selves in his holy presence are we ready for him to begin to work in us both to will and to do his good pleasure (cf. Phil. 2:13). We have nothing to offer God but our need. And we owe even our coming to that point of brokenness to his gracious work in our lives.

When any church or group sets itself up as the "one and only true," that church or group begins to choke spiritually on its own self-centeredness. Frank Laubach notes that the tendency to shut out the validity of God's work in others is natural to us all:

A great many saints are blocked also because they try to hold God to only one channel. . . . We all tend to shut ourselves out from God's myriad channels because we insist on God flowing down though our particular denominational or social or political channel. The dryness of many a saint has resulted from his closing off every pipeline except one. It is dreadful how sectarianism makes men consider goodness sinful unless it flows down their own ecclesiastical ditch![13]

How tragically true Laubach's words were in the Worldwide Church of God. We could not learn from the rich legacy of the Spirit's work in Christian history because we could not see God at work in any historical "pipeline" except that of what church headquarters deemed to consist of seventh-day Sabbatarians. Thank God for the redeeming and transforming power of his Word and his Spirit, who cannot be silenced or shackled!

CHURCH GOVERNMENT ACCORDING TO ARMSTRONG

In the Worldwide Church of God, Herbert Armstrong, within the bounds of the law, held final authority on all matters, doctrinal and administrative. Though, like any citizen, Armstrong was accountable to the law of the land, and though he was legally accountable to the board of directors, he had no sense of personal accountability to the church board or any other eccle-siastical entity. His explanation was that he was accountable to the "highest authority," that is, to God. God had set him in the position of "physical head of the church under Christ," and he was accountable to Christ alone, not to any man.

In his self-appointed capacity as "end-time apostle," Armstrong interpreted the Scriptures and decided church doctrine according to his own understanding and comfort level. He was collaborative on any given point of doctrine, policy, or adminis-tration only to the degree he saw fit. Collaboration and account-ability, except when legally required, were purely matters of his personal preference or choice. Even when Armstrong was col-laborative on doctrinal issues, it was clear to all church officials, ministers, and members that the final authority and decision belonged to him and him alone.

Herbert Armstrong's stranglehold on doctrine, particularly his Sabbatarianism, necessarily had a profound impact on worship in the Worldwide Church of God, as we will see in Chapter 5.

Herbert W. Armstrong promoting The Plain Truth *on a* World Tomorrow *television program late in his life.*

A Case of Mistaken
Identity

IN DECEMBER 1994 THE Worldwide Church of God changed its doctrine on the seventh-day Sabbath and the seven annual festivals of Leviticus 23. Since its formation in 1933, the church had believed and taught vigorously that observance of the seventh-day Sabbath and the seven annual holy days was required for Christians and that the only true Christians were Sabbath and holy day keepers.

The Sabbath and holy day doctrine had been at the core of the church's sense of identity, and for many members its abandonment was devastating. "How can we be the true church anymore?" many asked. Besides the call to proclaim the gospel, the church had felt an equal sense of mission to proclaim the Sabbath and holy days to the "falsely so-called Christians" of other Christian churches. For Herbert Armstrong's church, the Sabbath and the gospel could not be separated.

The tragedy of Herbert Armstrong's Sabbatarian and annual holy day system was that it formed a mask for true righteousness. As an obedient Sabbath keeper, one is able to appear and even feel quite righteous, quite honorable before God because of adherence to laws one believes to be the definition of godly living.

TURNING WORSHIP INTO WORKS

By its very definition in the Worldwide Church of God as the true sign of God's people, the requirement to be faithful in Sabbath and holy day observance led members to place greater emphasis on their performance than on Jesus Christ. When the sign of God's people is the Sabbath, then the sign of God's people cannot be something else. Specifically, it cannot be love for one another.[1] In the Worldwide Church of God, consequently, leaders defined Christian love as faithfulness to the law—in particular, faithfulness to the Sabbath and the holy days. Therefore, in the Worldwide Church of God, worship itself was focused on the act of keeping the Sabbath and the holy days.

When Christians come together in worship, they are responding to the grace and power of God in their individual and corporate lives. This is the essence of Christian worship: the response of the people of God to what God has done. The worship of ancient Israel centered on what God had done for them—delivering them from slavery in Egypt by opening the Red Sea, preserving them in the wilderness, and bringing them into the land of promise. The forms of worship God gave them were designed to enable them to respond appropriately to the great acts of God on their behalf.

A New Act Demands a New Response

Just as Isaiah had prophesied, at the fullness of time God did a *new thing* (Isa. 43:19)—he sent his Son. The response of the people of God to this new thing is a fitting *new response*. New response to a new thing demands new worship *content*, content that must be carried out in appropriately new *forms*. In other words, the *new wine* of the gospel of Jesus Christ is to be placed into *new wineskins*.

For Christians who are religiously committed to certain forms of old covenant worship, such as Sabbatarians, it can be a daunting challenge to come to grips with the fact that it was *Jesus* who set the pace for developing a worship pattern that depicts fulfillment of old covenant rituals *in him*. Since worship is the response of God's people to his mighty acts of salvation and grace, the content and form of worship is a direct reflection of the fundamental beliefs of God's people.[2]

A comparison of the biblical creeds of the people of God under the old and the new covenants (see Figure 1) illustrates the passing of the old and the arrival of the new. The old covenant people of God remembered and celebrated the great power and grace of God displayed in their miraculous deliverance from slavery in Egypt and in the gift of the land promised to the patriarchs. The new covenant people of God, on the other hand, remember and celebrate the great power and grace of God displayed in the life, death, and resurrection of Jesus Christ. The content and form of their worship reflects their belief that through confidence in Jesus *all peoples everywhere* can be delivered from slavery to sin and given entrance into the new life of the kingdom of God.

FIGURE 1: CREEDS OF THE OLD AND NEW COVENANTS[3]

Biblical Creeds of Israel Reflected in Its Worship	Biblical Creeds of the Church Reflected in Its Worship
"Then you shall declare before the LORD your God: 'My father was a wandering Aramean, and he went down into Egypt with a few people and lived there and became a great nation, powerful and numerous. But the Egyptians mistreated us and made us suffer, putting us to hard labor. Then we cried out to the LORD, the God of our fathers, and the LORD heard our voice and saw our misery, toil and oppression. So the LORD brought us out of	"For what I received I passed on to you as of first importance: that Christ died for our sins according to the Scriptures, that he was buried, that he was raised on the third day according to the Scriptures, that he appeared to Peter, and then to the Twelve." 1 Corinthians 15:3–5 "He appeared in a body, was vindicated by the Spirit, was seen by angels, was preached among the

Egypt with a mighty hand and an outstretched arm, with great terror and with miraculous signs and wonders. He brought us to this place and gave us this land, a land flowing with milk and honey.'"

Deuteronomy 26:5–9

"Tell him: 'We were slaves of Pharaoh in Egypt, but the LORD brought us out of Egypt with a mighty hand. Before our eyes the LORD sent miraculous signs and wonders—great and terrible— upon Egypt and Pharaoh and his whole household. But he brought us out from there to bring us in and give us the land that he promised on oath to our forefathers. The LORD commanded us to obey all these decrees and to fear the LORD our God, so that we might always prosper and be kept alive, as is the case today. And if we are careful to obey all this law before the LORD our God, as he has commanded us, that will be our righteousness.'"

Deuteronomy 6:21–25

nations, was believed on in the world, was taken up in glory."

1 Timothy 3:16

"Who, being in very nature God, did not consider equality with God something to be grasped, but made himself nothing, taking the very nature of a servant, being made in human likeness. And being found in appearance as a man, he humbled himself and became obedient to death—even death on a cross!
Therefore God exalted him to the highest place and gave him the name that is above every name, that at the name of Jesus every knee should bow, in heaven and on earth and under the earth, and every tongue confess that Jesus Christ is Lord, to the glory of God the Father."

Philippians 2:6–11

NEW FESTIVALS CELEBRATE A NEW EXODUS

Christian worship involves *new* festivals because it celebrates the *new* exodus—an exodus from slavery to sin for all humankind—

not the old Exodus, which was an exodus from slavery in Egypt for the people of Israel. The historical commitment of the Worldwide Church of God to a pattern of worship that eschewed "pagan Christian holidays" while it celebrated old covenant festivals, which by definition memorialize the Exodus event, could not help but hinder members' full and free celebration of Jesus Christ as the fulfillment of all God's promises and the ultimate hope of all humanity. In worship, Christians do not merely look back to a historical event. Rather, as Robert Webber explains, "Worship is the action that brings the Christ event into the experience of the community gathered in the name of Jesus. . . . In worship we rehearse the Gospel story."[4] Regardless of *when* Christians finally choose to gather, the real issue is whether their celebration becomes a *genuine rehearsal of the gospel story.*

SOURING WORSHIP WITH LEGALISM

Herbert Armstrong was adamant that one cannot be saved apart from Sabbath keeping. He wrote:

> Did you realize that Christ Himself said you cannot only profess His name and call yourself a Christian, but you may actually WORSHIP HIM—*and do it in vain?* Still totally "unsaved"?
>
> Listen to the very words of Christ: "Howbeit *in vain* do they worship me, teaching for doctrines the commandments of men. For laying aside the commandment of God, ye hold the tradition of men . . . ye reject the commandment of God, that ye may keep your own tradition" (Mark 7:7–9).
>
> Assembling for worship on Sunday is *nothing but the tradition of* MEN—and a pagan tradition at that! Those who do so *reject the Commandment of* GOD, disobey God's Commandment to *keep* His Sabbath day holy, are guilty of COMMITTING SIN, and SUCH WORSHIP IS UTTERLY IN VAIN! *Jesus Christ said so!*[5]

Regardless of anything biblically sound and spiritually sensible Armstrong may have taught or written, any time the Sabbatarian card was played, everything else was trumped. All matters of identity, faithfulness, and salvation ultimately came down to Sabbath keeping.

What it amounted to was this: You could not be saved without Christ *and* the Sabbath. If you did not have the Sabbath, nothing could save you, because by Sabbatarian logic, if you do not have the Sabbath, you cannot possibly have Christ. The blood of Christ only flows for Sabbath keepers. Armstrong put it this way:

> Now *IF* Jesus Christ is *IN YOU* (and you are not a truly converted Christian unless He is!) will He, *in you*, profane His Holy Day, and observe a pagan day? *IMPOSSIBLE!*
>
> Jesus Christ has not changed. He is THE SAME, yesterday, today, and forever! (Heb. 13:8).
>
> It is CHRIST who *made* the Sabbath. It is CHRIST who rested on that very first Sabbath! It is the ETERNAL (Yahweh) who became the Christ who spoke to the Israelites on the Sabbath (Ex. 16). It is CHRIST who kept the Sabbath *as His custom was* (Luke 4:16).
>
> Jesus Christ has always *put His Presence* in His own Holy Day! *IF* Christ is *IN* you—He, in you, can keep no other day NOW! And *IF* you, having read the truth in this booklet, now make excuse, or rebel, and refuse to *keep* holy Christ's Holy Day, then on His infallible authority, I say to you that He is not IN you!
>
> It is just that serious![6]

Armstrong concluded his Sabbath booklet with this dire warning:

> It is now UP to *YOU!*
>
> I have given you God's Word faithfully. It is not popular. It is not what the popular majority tell you.

But NOW you *KNOW!* You will be JUDGED by what you do with this knowledge!

You must make your own choice. Rebellion means eternal PUNISHMENT of everlasting DEATH. God will *save* no person He does not RULE.

You must choose between God's ways, and MAN'S ways he falsely calls "Christian."

My responsibility ends with TELLING you. I have cried aloud. I have lifted my voice. I have TOLD YOU YOUR SIN in this regard. God calls *you* to repentance. But He will not force you. You must make your own decision, and what you sow you shall reap.

You shall be saved by GRACE, but God does lay down conditions. You can comply, and receive glorious GRACE—or you can rebel, and pay the DEATH PENALTY—for eternity![7]

In Armstrong's Worldwide Church of God, right worship consisted primarily of meeting on the *right* days and, equally important, not meeting on the *wrong* days. To meet faithfully on the seventh-day Sabbath and the seven annual Israelite holy days was to worship rightly. To meet on Sunday or to celebrate Easter and Christmas was to worship wrongly—to sin.

Worship was *obedience to the law,* pure and simple. To love God was precisely to obey the law, especially the Sabbath command.

It is not that grace, hope, and the potential for forgiveness were absent from the preaching and teaching of Armstrong's church. It is that they were stifled and tainted by the pervasive and grace-destroying Sabbatarianism, which bred legalism. Preaching in Armstrong's church alluded to grace, but it abounded with condemnation, judgmentalism, and self-absorption.

SELF-CENTERED FIXATION

The focus of Armstrong's church was consistently on itself—its conduct, its faithfulness, and its identity as the only true church. One of the major "proofs" that Armstrong's church was the "one and only true church" was the fact that it observed the seventh-day Sabbath and the "biblical" holy days. Worship on the right days was at least as much a means of establishing the identity of the church as God's only faithful as it was a means of bringing glory and honor to God. *We were God's people, and other so-called "Christians" were not;* and this was true because we kept the right days. Armstrong wrote: "We have a history of the true Church of God through every century from Christ until now. It has always been a SABBATH-KEEPING Church."[8]

Our coming together was a testament to *our identity* more than it was a testament to *God's identity.* "Why are we here?" Herbert Armstrong would preach on each annual holy day. The consistent answer went something like this: "We are here because God commands it; we are the only people who obey God by being here; we are the only true church; we must never lose these holy days, or we won't be God's people any more; we are the only ones who know God's plan, because only by keeping these holy days that God restored through me can anyone know God's plan."

Worship in the Worldwide Church of God was out of gas before it could get the car out of the garage. How can a church celebrate the incarnation of the self-sacrificial God when it cannot get past its fixation on who is in or out of the kingdom of God based on obedience to laws governing obsolete holy days?

After condemning all churches that meet on Sunday as the "harlot daughters" of the great whore (the mother Roman church), one of the early booklets of Armstrong's church asserted: "The Bible does not say we are to assemble with the world, but with OURSELVES—*those who are truly converted.* God has *not* convoked weekly religious meetings on Sunday morning!"[9] To be absolutely clear that not just *any* Sabbath-keeping church will do, the booklet continues: "Neither are we to assemble on Saturday with an apostatizing Church which sees the *argument* about the Sabbath but which follows the false visions of a woman 'prophetess' and rejects the gospel of *the kingdom of God.*"[10]

So what must a person do to truly "have communion and fellowship" with Christ? The booklet answers: "Withdraw at once from all other fellowship, except that of CHRIST, and those who are IN CHRIST, and Christ IN THEM."[11] Since the Armstrong church was the only church body in which the Holy Spirit dwelled (on the basis of its Sabbath and holy day observance, along with its proclamation of the "true gospel"), one could only find fellowship with Christ, and therefore salvation, in Armstrong's church.

To bathe oneself in the holy presence of God was considered absurd. What God wanted was obedience to the law, pure and simple. Prayer was to be primarily oriented toward repentance for lawbreaking, help for obedience, requests for personal needs and the needs of others, and intercession for "the Work," that is, for Herbert and Garner Ted Armstrong,[12] for the media outreach on radio, television, and publishing, and for the ministers and headquarters in general. Members were taught that prayer should include praise and thanksgiving, but the idea of coming silently into the presence of God for pure worship and adoration, for example, was not a subject that occurred to many members or ministers. Prayer was "our communication with God," and Bible study was "God's communication with us." Consequently, prayer time was talking time, not listening time.

SMALL-GROUP WORSHIP NOT PERMITTED

Herbert Armstrong was clear that all worship in any context besides the Sabbath-keeping church he founded was completely in vain. But he took his distortion of corporate worship even one step further. Members of the Worldwide Church of God were specifically taught *not* to pray or worship in small groups. Members were not even to gather for Bible study, much less for prayer and worship, without an ordained minister present. The 1959 church booklet, *A True History of the True Church*, instructs:

> In John 15:5, Jesus said: "I am the vine, ye are the branches." What would you think if the branches would say

to themselves, let us bundle ourselves together? That is exactly what you are doing when you meet *of your own accord without a minister!* . . . We baptize "in the name of Jesus Christ"—"by His authority." But Jesus never gave authority for His converts to hold meetings by themselves without a pastor! Any who do so are not acting according to Jesus' commands. They are going contrary to Christ's authority. He does not promise to be in their midst.[13]

What were adherents to Armstrongism to do if there were no pastor in their area? The same booklet answers: "But we are not actually left without fellowship. When the World Tomorrow Broadcast[14] is on the air, you are attending, in a sense, a church service *with a minister.* This is how God is feeding many in his flock."[15] Once again, worship is relegated to the role of a tool to uphold Herbert Armstrong as God's appointed end-time apostle and Armstrong's church as the one and only true church, the body to which one *must* belong in order to be saved.

C. Welton Gaddy writes, "Christian worship embraces and celebrates the incarnation of God in Jesus Christ. . . . To attempt the worship of God for any other purpose than glorifying God compromises worship."[16]For Herbert Armstrong's church, however, worship embraced and celebrated its obedience to the law of God, its superior knowledge of the plan of God that it believed was revealed only in the annual Israelite holy days, and its identity as the only true church.

TRUTH DEMANDS HONESTY

According to Frederick Buechner, the key to effective preaching is honesty.[17] And as Buechner asserts, the incarnation is the epitome of honesty. That is because Jesus Christ—God with us, God in the flesh—ever faithful, meets us precisely where we are—in a particular place at a particular time in the particular reality of our broken and wretched humanity. He offers himself as the perfect means to our healing and restoration, and he perfectly establishes in himself our eternal significance and future.

We are made in such a way that this astounding truth reaches our hearts through the stimulation of our imagination—not through the logical "proofs" and stacks of facts we like to amass before we are prepared to believe anything that threatens to significantly change the way we live. And Buechner is surely right about the sheer wildness of this story. It is an extravagant tale—at once shocking, disturbing, comforting, and thrilling. It is a paradox of unbounded power and senseless self-sacrifice, a song of indescribable love in the face of brutal disaster. It is the turning and twisting story of the crucible of our confusing lives into which God himself has entered to bring meaning to the absurd.

Always surprising, always unexpected, always turning the endlessly resurfacing tragedy to hope, always piercing turmoil with peace, always wringing joy out of pain, this gospel is the root and fountainhead of all the human story, the mysterious reality from which all forms of the human story flow. In the gospel everything changes, yet everything continues as it was before. In the gospel of Jesus Christ the impossible is possible though it cannot be done, and the darkness is lit with invisible light. As Fredrick Buechner so richly puts it, this gospel is "the tale that is too good not to be true."[18]

That, I believe, is precisely the tragedy of Herbert Armstrong's self-conceived worship calendar. Misunderstanding the very Bible he accepted as his authority, and rejecting the witness of the Holy Spirit in the history of the Christian church, Armstrong designed his own hybrid version of the old covenant worship forms. Locked firmly into a system of worship designed by God for the express purpose of helping the Israelites rehearse and celebrate their exodus from Egypt, Armstrong's church could not help but miss something of the glory and majesty of the incarnation.

FINDING ROOM FOR DIVERSITY

James White seems to be speaking to the precise situation confronting the Worldwide Church of God as it moves from its former worldwide lockstep approach to worship styles and patterns to a flexible pattern worked out at the level of each local congregation. White argues, "Perhaps we should do more to encourage diversity rather than to seek consensus."[19]

Members of the Worldwide Church of God are sorely divided over the issue of whether to meet on the traditional WCG Israelite festivals or the traditional Christian festivals. Yet few members today seem to question the fact that *Jesus Christ* should be the center and focus of worship when we meet. Since this is the case, it would seem that White's plea for encouraging diversity would be consistent with the scriptural call to unity and Christian forbearance.

"Increasingly," White observes, "it seems that efforts by so-called liturgical law to make a single pattern of worship dominate are anachronistic."[20] For the Worldwide Church of God, this is certainly true. For the church to attempt to enforce a single pattern of worship at this time would be to force a major church split, and for what valid reason? White points out that "the churches exist from the grassroots up and usually liturgical decisions should be made at the lowest level possible. Pastoral discretion has been with us at least since Justin Martyr."[21] The very fact that Christian worship *developed* through the witness of the Holy Spirit to Jesus Christ rather than having been prescribed like the worship of Israel would seem to validate White's argument.

The worldwide, international flavor of the Worldwide Church of God makes the need for pastoral discretion in matters of worship all the more critical. "The God whom we worship seems to relish diversity,"[22] White says. If that is so, as it certainly must be, then the Worldwide Church of God is proceeding on safe theological ground as it begins to encourage *locally relevant* and *soundly Christ-centered* worship in its local congregations, regardless of the particular days on which individual congregations may choose to gather.[23]

"FOUR TO SEVEN SHORT YEARS"

WHEN I FIRST READ the expanded version of Herbert Armstrong's *United States and British Commonwealth in Prophecy*, I was sixteen years old and working at the WCG summer camp for teens in Orr, Minnesota. Those of us who had been selected from the church's Imperial High School to serve as summer camp workers were housed in our own dorm and given our own counselor. A stack of freshly printed copies of the new updated and expanded version of *US and BC*, as we affectionately called it, was provided so that each of us could have our own copy for study. I was struck by the deliberately oversized words of the opening paragraph:

> A STAGGERING TURN in world events is due to erupt in the next four to seven years. It will involve violently the United States, Britain, Western Europe, the Middle East.[1]

My sixteen-year-old imagination was stirred by the large phrase "in the next four to seven years." That would make me, as I counted it, twenty to twenty-three. It was scary. It was exciting. And it was good to have the inside knowledge about something so astounding, something only the very elect of God were privileged to know.

"Time is short," we heard nearly every week at church. "Time is running out!" Well, of course, time *did* run out—on Armstrong's prediction of four to seven years, that is, as it had on all his other time-bound predictions. When would the lesson ever be learned—by Armstrong *or* by his followers?

The trail of failed predictions reads like a *Saturday Night Live* skit. Consider just the sampling in Figure 2 below.

Figure 2: Sample Worldwide Church of God Failed Predictions

Prediction	Date Printed
Combining the many, many other prophecies of the great tribulation . . . we may be absolutely certain that we are in, and for about three years have been passing through, this great world-wide tribulation.	*The Plain Truth,* February 1934
But this you MAY KNOW! This war [WWII] will be ended by CHRIST'S RETURN! And MAY start within six weeks! We are just THAT NEAR Christ's coming!	*The Plain Truth,* August 1939
IT'S TIME THIS NATION *KNEW* WHAT LIES IN STORE FOR IT DURING THE NEXT 5, 10, AND 15 years— years destined to be FAR MORE MOMENTOUS THAN ANYTHING WE HAVE LIVED THRU SO FAR! IT'S TIME FOR *YOU* to WAKE UP!	*The Plain Truth,* March 1950
It is now definitely proved that Adolph Hitler did not die in his Berlin bunker at the close of World War II, as reported to the world. Evidence points persistently to the fact he was flown by private plane to a waiting submarine, and taken to a fantastic Shangri-la hide-out known to have been prepared by the Nazis in the wastes of Antarctica.	*The Good News,* May 1954
These terrifying world-shaking events will take place in less than thirty years—in your lifetime, this very last generation that is destined to live in two worlds!	*The Plain Truth,* September 1955

It is time we recognized that civilization has not more than 15 years to go unless a supernatural God in Heaven intervenes on earth to stop mad men from destroying all life on earth in their crazed dreams for world conquest.	*The Plain Truth,* February 1965
Frankly, literally dozens of prophesied events indicate that this final revival of the Roman Empire in Europe— and its bestial PERSECUTION of multitudes of Bible-believing Christians—will take place within the next seven to ten years of YOUR LIFE!	*The Plain Truth,* February 1965
I told you it could happen in the 1980s, or 1990s. Now I tell you it COULD (I do not yet say will) happen in a year! I would not be surprised to see it beginning to go together before the end of this year. Fifteen years ago I thought our Work might be finished by 1972. But God seemed to DELAY the end of this present world by eight or ten years. But now the prophesied events indicate we are at the time of Romans 9:28: "For He will finish the work, and cut it short in righteousness; because a short work will the Lord make upon the earth."	Semi-Annual Letter to All Subscribers, June 1980
As I write, the greater part of the British fleet that once "ruled the waves" of the whole world, in one vast armada is arriving just off the Falkland Islands, ready for WAR. DON'T BE SURPRISED IF THE BRITISH FLEET IS DESTROYED IN THE NEXT FEW DAYS! Gibraltar will come next, and already is in danger.	Member Letter, August 1983
We have already been a very few years into the pre-lude of the GREAT TRIBULATION. That is virtually upon us now.	Member Letter, September 1984

Every sign tells us these things will happen, plunging the world into the most frantic, frenzied state of anguish ever known, almost certainly within a matter of the next several years.	*The Good News,* October/November 1985

"Woodenheadedness"

It is amazing how long a ministry can keep up the façade of prophetic prediction. There is always a convenient excuse when the prescribed number of years comes and goes, and the true believers always seem to fall for it. One of the most clever is to blame it on the lack of spiritual growth in the members. In this way, the failed prediction is not the fault of the church leader; it is the fault of the people he is deceiving. "God has delayed the timing because you members are not yet ready." Armstrong used that one well.

He also used this one: "God has given us a little more time to get out our warning message." And this one: "We didn't calculate the 'times of the gentiles' correctly." And my personal favorite: "We forgot about the seven years of Nebuchadnezzar's insanity." That one bought us seven more years after the great failure of Armstrong's prediction that the Great Tribulation would begin in 1972.

Nearly every prayer in our church ended with the words: "And we pray all these things in the name of our High Priest and *soon-coming* King, Jesus Christ." The concept of the "soon coming" of Christ was fused into our collective psyche. "Soon-coming King" was as much a title for Jesus as Lord and Savior. For one thing, Herbert Armstrong taught that Jesus was *not yet* king. He would only become king at his Second Coming, according to Armstrong. But the Second Coming was definitely *soon*, because Armstrong was God's man, specially raised up to preach to the "final, end-time generation" before Christ's return.

Walter Kaiser Jr. decries the penchant for date setting that many sincere Christians today have:

> For every ten believers who are reluctant to study prophecy, there is one zealot whose love for the subject is exceeded only by a penchant for being cocksure about every identification he or she makes, including the date for every event slated for the future. In fact, we will not even need to press these zealots to tell us the exact date for the second coming of our Lord. Yes, they know that the Bible says that even our Lord did not know the time, but what they propose to tell us is not the "time," but only the week or the year! What can one say to such wooden-headedness? These are the people who give prophecy its bad press and who discourage others from its legitimate pursuit.[2]

Herbert Armstrong and his followers were not alone in their fascination with end-time prophecy and the date of Jesus' return. It was precisely this fascination, coupled with Armstrong's dogmatic confidence, that gave Armstrong's *The World Tomorrow* radio program and *The Plain Truth* magazine, along with his book *The United States and British Commonwealth in Prophecy*, such explosive popularity. All told, nearly 6 million copies of *The United States and British Commonwealth in Prophecy* were printed and distributed between 1948 and 1986. At its zenith, *The World Tomorrow* radio program was airing somewhere in the world at virtually any time day or night; and at its height, circulation of *The Plain Truth* topped 8 million.

EXPLOITATION

With his characteristic style of hyperbolic overstatement, Armstrong staked the validity of the Bible itself on his interpretation of the identity of the modern descendants of Ephraim and Manasseh. He wrote:

The COVENANT PROMISE to David is plain and definite.

Either his dynasty has continued, and exists today, ruling over the House of ISRAEL (not the Jews), or God's Word fails! . . .

Has the sceptre departed from Judah?

Has the throne ceased? Or does it, as God so bindingly promised, exist today so that Christ can take over and sit upon a living, going, continuous throne when He comes?

The infallibility of the Bible is at stake! God's WORD is at stake![3]

The throne to which Armstrong was referring is the throne of the United Kingdom, specifically that of Queen Elizabeth II, which Armstrong believed to be the continuation of the throne of David. The infallibility of the Bible was not at stake, of course. The only thing at stake was the validity of Armstrong's Bible-defying interpretation.

To Armstrong the modern identity of the Israelite tribes was the "master key" to understanding all of Bible prophecy. Not only that, but Armstrong's dogmatism on this doctrine extended to a declaration that it was the *strongest proof* of the inspiration of the Bible and the *strongest proof* of the existence of God:

But the all-important MASTER KEY has been found!

That KEY is knowledge of the astonishing identity of the American and British peoples—as well as the German—in Bible prophecies.

This very eye-opening, astounding IDENTITY is the strongest PROOF of the inspiration and authority of the Holy Bible! It is at the same time, the *strongest* proof of the very active existence of THE LIVING GOD![4]

How sure was Armstrong that his "specially revealed" interpretation was true, that his date-setting predictions were accurate, and that his unique warning message was vitally important? He wrote: "The events prophesied to strike the American and British peoples in the next four to seven years are SURE! That is why events of the next four to seven years may prove this to be the most significant book of this century."[5]

Richard Foster urged Christian leaders: *"Please, for God's sake, refuse to exploit the hopes and fears of your people with speculative prophecy preaching."*[6] Such exploitation is precisely what Herbert Armstrong practiced.

In the May 15, 1990, issue of the *Pastor General's Report*, Joseph Tkach Sr. countered Armstrong's "master key." He wrote: "The central core and theme of all our commission, all our Work and all our lives is Jesus Christ. It is not the specifics of end-time prophecy. It is not the identity of modern nations. It is not the identity of church eras."[7] In the May 28 issue, Tkach added, "We should preach continually about the return of Christ with eager anticipation. But we should not claim to know something that is, in reality, only speculation and opinion and then use Scripture to support our view."[8]

GOD SAVE US FROM OUR ALMIGHTY DISTINCTIVES

Pet doctrines are dangerous. They can easily crowd out the gospel itself, precisely because defending them requires so much energy. It is interesting that in the past few years many church leaders have advised us, "Don't lose your distinctives. Every church needs its distinctives." It's funny how worried church people can get about even the prospect of the erosion of this entity we call "distinctives."

After what we have been through, one has to wonder, What is the big deal about distinctives? I think it might be quite simple. For churches, our distinctives very quickly tend to become our identity. They are what mark us off as being unique from other Christians. They make us special, shape our unique mission, give us a sense of purpose, meaning, and cohesion. They take a lot of our time and energy. What is wrong with this picture?

Herbert Armstrong got so carried away with his pet doctrine about the modern identity of Israel that he frequently overstated it profoundly. This is the normal path that "special teachings" and "unique revelations" tend to take unless deliberate care is taken to prevent it. Precisely because they set their adherents apart from the rest of Christians, such distinctives create a temptation for Christians to promote them to center stage in defense and proclamation. An example of this unhappy phenomenon in Armstrong's case is the sentence I have underlined in this excerpt from Armstrong's *The United States and British Commonwealth in Prophecy:*

> The very fate of the Bible as the revealed Word of God—the evidence of the existence of God—hangs on the answer to this momentous question [the question of which nations today are the modern descendants of the so-called lost ten tribes of Israel]. The Jewish people did not fulfill these promises. They do not refer to the Church. The world with its great church leaders does not know of any such fulfillment. Did God fail? Or has He made good this colossal promise unknown to the world?
>
> <u>The true answer is the most astonishing revelation of Bible truth, of prophecy, and of unrecognized history!</u>[19]

Obviously, the incarnation of the Son of God for the salvation of human beings is the most astonishing revelation of Bible truth, not Herbert Armstrong's Anglo-Israelism. The identity that matters is that of Jesus Christ, not that of the United States and Britain.

Perhaps if the obvious problem with statements like this one had been pointed out to Armstrong directly, he would have heartily agreed and rewritten them. However, that did not happen, and the zeal, vigor, and force with which he taught and defended this pet doctrine resulted in colossal overstatement amounting to colossal heresy. Not only did Armstrong completely misunderstand the promise passages he employed to defend his Anglo-Israel doctrine, but his false (and borrowed[10]) interpretation clouded and obscured their true meaning and their true fulfillment in Jesus Christ.

COPING WITH THE ROLE OF THE FOUNDER

It is difficult to read this and the previous chapters without wondering how WCG members cope with the role of their church founder. Some fellow Christians, mainly of the cult-watching variety, cannot seem to find rest until the reformed Worldwide Church of God publicly brands Herbert Armstrong as a damnable false prophet worthy of being stoned to death. Others are more gracious. Regardless of the dust-throwing, attention-grabbing antics of certain cult-watchers, the question remains: How does a WCG member deal with the Herbert Armstrong question?

Barrier to Christ

Who was Herbert W. Armstrong anyway? He has been described in many ways by many people: as a faithful, if imperfect, man of God; as a successful evangelist who brought thousands to faith in Christ, even if their understanding was incomplete; as a basically sincere but theologically unsophisticated man who got a few, or quite a few, details wrong; as a colossal heretic; as a shrewd advertising man who found an especially productive marketplace in hawking religion; as a dishonest control freak who used religion to get the lifestyle he wanted; as an authoritarian egomaniac who honestly believed he was the most important man on the planet; as a religious hypocrite par excellence, who demanded absolute obedience and loyalty of his followers but routinely broke his own rules.

At various times I have seen Herbert Armstrong in at least all of these ways. Sometimes in a matter of days I have swung from admiration to anger, from respect to revulsion, from praise to pity to disgust. One thing is for sure: Herbert Armstrong's judgment is not my business; it is the Lord's. Another thing is for sure: members and former members of the Worldwide Church of God, including myself, have to cope with the question of who Herbert Armstrong was and get past him in order to come to Jesus Christ.

I firmly believe that as long as people continue to believe that Armstrong was what he claimed to be, they cannot fully enjoy the rich assurance, rest, and joy of salvation that is theirs through confidence in Jesus. To me, that is the crux of the Herbert Armstrong question: Was he what he claimed to be? And the answer, the "plain truth," is that he was not.

Not What He Claimed to Be

In order to come to a full and confident assurance of salvation by grace through faith, Armstrongites have to let go of Herbert Armstrong. *He was not what he claimed to be.* He was not "the Elijah to come." He was not "Zerubbabel." He was not "a voice crying out in the wilderness of religious confusion." He was not "preparing the way for the soon-coming return of Jesus Christ." He did not "restore all things." He was not "raised up to proclaim the end-time message." He was not "God's only true messenger in the end-time." He was not "God's only true apostle on earth." He did not "raise up the only true end-time church." *He was not what he claimed to be.*

Herbert Armstrong did found the Worldwide Church of God. That will always be the historical fact. And he did preach that Jesus Christ died for human sin, was raised from the dead for our salvation, and is our High Priest and Advocate. He did preach that there is no salvation apart from faith in Jesus Christ. He did preach "Don't believe me, believe your Bible." And he did change a doctrinal point more than once because he believed the Bible demanded it, despite the humiliation and opposition created by the change.

At the same time, Herbert Armstrong undeniably had an inflated opinion of himself and the importance of his work. He taught that nobody could be saved unless he or she was in the church he founded. He taught that nobody was a true Christian unless he or she kept the Saturday Sabbath and the Israelite holy days. In one of his Bible studies on the book of First Corinthians in 1980, Armstrong defended a disagreement with the apostle Paul about marriage on the basis of his belief that he was equal to Paul in apostolic authority.[11]

Unrelenting Condemnation

If *what* Armstrong taught was not bad enough, *how* he taught it was even worse. As many researchers have pointed out in accusing Armstrong of plagiarism, you can find most, if not all, of Armstrong's doctrinal errors in theory or practice in other- wise "orthodox" Christian churches. The problem was Arm- strong's unrelenting contention that everyone who was not in his church was not Christian. It was his complete condemnation of everyone who disagreed with him that was so pernicious and spiritually damaging. It was his view of himself as "God's only true apostle today," his view of his church as the "only true church," and the natural implications of those perspectives that created a barrier to coming fully into the freedom of the gospel. What led to such outrageous (speaking in hindsight) conclu- sions? For one thing, it was Armstrong's Sabbatarianism.

The Real Sabbath

I will go so far as to say that Sabbatarianism[12] prevents any- one who believes in it from coming fully to the freedom of the gospel. I know my Sabbatarian friends will strongly disagree. I used to strongly disagree, too. "We know Jesus died for our sins," I said. "We know all our righteousness is only filthy rags," I said. "We know we can only be saved by Jesus' righteousness attributed to us," I said. Some Sabbatarians even say they know there are converted non-Sabbatarians. But when you really press an honest Sabbatarian, he will finally have to admit that he believes a saved person will someday, somehow finally come to be a Sabbath-keeper. He cannot affirm that a person can finally be saved and never be a Sabbath-keeper in this life or the next. Like it or not, to believe that salvation finally comes only to Sabbath-keepers means you have not come fully to the gospel.

When you accept the gospel fully, you know that legalistic Sabbath keeping is irrelevant to salvation. You know that *Jesus* is, in fact, your Sabbath. You know that your eternal rest is in him, and that it is entered by faith in him, by believing the gospel, by believing in him. You know that obedience to the law has nothing at all to do with your salvation. You know that your only hope is in what God has done for your salvation and that God has bought you through the saving work of Jesus. Sabbatarianism has no role; it has no value at all, in any sense, to the gospel. The legal Sabbath was only a pointer, like circumcision, to what would become real in Jesus. The weekly Sabbath is no more crucial to your relationship with God than your wedding chapel rental contract is to your relationship with your spouse.

Herbert Armstrong "did things up right," I've heard many people say. He also did Sabbatarianism up right. He took it where it logically belongs. If God commands it, Armstrong taught, you'd better keep it. And if you don't, you are in rebellion against God. What's wrong with this picture? Only one thing: God *doesn't* command it for Christians.

The Sabbath, along with the rest of the law, was given to *Moses*, for *Israel*, on *Mount Sinai*. It was a sign of the covenant between God and Israel. It was not given to the whole world. It was not given to the church. It was not given to Christians. It was not a sign between God and Christians. The last verse of the book of Leviticus makes it "so simple a child could understand":[13] "These are the commands the LORD gave Moses on Mount Sinai for the Israelites" (Lev. 27:34).

SUFFICIENCY OF THE BLOOD

Just how much grace does God have? Does he have enough grace for Herbert Armstrong? Several self-appointed cult-watchers don't think so. But I do. I think God has enough grace for all sinners. I think Herbert Armstrong was a sinner and that he taught a good-sized chunk of heresy. I think he misled a lot of people, including me, about a lot of important things. But I think that Jesus loves him and that Jesus died for him. Despite his sins and his theological ignorance and even his arrogance, Herbert Armstrong believed that Jesus Christ was the Son of God[14] and that Jesus died for his sins. Now, either salvation is by grace through faith or it is not. And if the cult-watchers don't think it is, then the cult-watchers must have their own set of special rules for salvation.

Does the blood of Jesus cover even bad theology? For some people, I know, that is a hard question. But when you've been the self-appointed judge and jury of all Christianity only to be knocked to the ground by the risen Christ, when you've been a confirmed legalist and then one day you find your Savior picking you off the ground and pouring a long draught of his grace down your sin-parched throat, it all becomes pretty simple.

Salvation comes by the grace of God. Through Jesus Christ, God has done everything it takes to save you, bad theology and all, and you can trust yourself to him. The Worldwide Church of God is regularly approached about becoming some kind of cult-watching center. I pray we never descend again to thinking ourselves the legitimate arbiters of truth versus error. Madeleine L'Engle put it well when she wrote:

> The people who accused Jesus of casting out devils by the Devil frighten me. The people who are looking to see if they can accuse someone of being in league with the Devil frighten me, too. . . .
>
> The terrible difference between us, the bride of Christ, and the tragic brides who are beaten by their husbands, is that it is we, ourselves, who are doing the battering. With

our warring denominations we have scratched at each others' eyes, pummeled and punched each other and ourselves, and so disgraced our host. What kind of a bruised and bloodied face do we show to the world? What kind of a bride of Christ do we make visible?

We will not become beautiful again until religion becomes a unifying and not a divisive word. We will not be beautiful again until we look for love, rather than Satan. We do find what we look for.[15]

Is that not true? When we look for the devil in others, we are sure to find what we are looking for. Who can stand against the relentless scrutiny of self-professed perfectionists? Is anyone faultless? Is any theological system completely invulnerable to an opposing point of view? Has God given any of us to see all things religious, moral, and theological in full and unfettered clarity, or was Paul actually correct when he said that we can only see through a cloudy glass?

Besides, there is One who does see all things with perfect clarity. He is the only one who has the right to condemn. Yet he chose to die, and he now lives so that sinners like me, like cultwatchers, and like Herbert Armstrong, might be saved through faith in his name.

Sinners and Saints

Was Herbert Armstrong a sinner or a saint? Certainly a sinner. But then, are not we all sinners? And are not we all—notwithstanding our imperfections, sins, ignorance, egotism, arrogance, and the lot—saints as well if we have confidence in the saving blood of Jesus? How wrong did Herbert Armstrong have to be in order to be considered unworthy of God's forgiving grace? How wrong does *anyone* have to be in order to be considered unworthy of God's grace? Who *is* worthy, after all? Are we not all unworthy of the gracious gift of salvation? Are cult-watchers more worthy of the grace of God than the doctrinally ignorant and infirm?

As Tom Torrance put it, "Jesus Christ died for you precisely because you are sinful and utterly unworthy of him."[16] How can we preach the gospel on one hand, yet not live with one another in love as though we really believe it on the other? Are we saved by grace through faith in Christ or not? Do we need, in fact, just a little more? In condemning Herbert Armstrong, who believed that Jesus was his Savior, to the flames of hell, are cult-watchers committing the same sin as Armstrong committed?

Don't we all, doctrinally "pure" and doctrinally odd alike, stand together at the foot of the cross, together in utter hopelessness and infinite need of God's amazing grace? Are not we all, at the end of the day, saved only by unfettered grace in helpless trust of the One who gives his bounteous wage without discrimination both to the workers who bore the heat of the day and to those who only show up at the last minute?

Maybe some cult-watchers become so busy looking for the devil in others that they fail to see that they have become what they are looking for—boundary erectors who make it their business to determine who is and who isn't worthy of the grace of God. That's just what cults do, of course. That's what the Worldwide Church of God did. In many ways, you could say the Worldwide Church of God was a cult-watching group. It established the true doctrine according to its interpretation of the Bible and set everyone who didn't embrace its established dogma outside the boundaries. Are some of the cult-watchers much different? As various Bible scholars have observed, it is the Bible that is infallible, not our interpretations of it.

"It's *déjà vu* all over again," Yogi Berra is supposed to have said. It is fascinating to consider that the only people Jesus roundly condemned were those whose religious beliefs, however correct, erected boundaries around the kingdom of God. When the Worldwide Church of God is asked—virtually commanded by some cult-watchers—to utterly condemn Herbert Armstrong, it is being asked to do what Jesus never did. It is being asked to draw boundaries around the potential of the grace of God to reach even into the area of doctrinal error. Yes, Herbert Armstrong taught error. But does not the grace of God extend even to doctrinal error? I have to believe it does.

That makes me think of one blustery preacher who said that Herbert Armstrong stands under God's damnation because of all the tens of thousands of souls whom he caused to go to hell by his preaching. Such reasoning is illogical and inconsistent when compared to the biblical descriptions of God. It is simply absurd to conceive of the God of the Bible as some puny, weak, hand-wringing, impotent deity who is so incompetent, even stupid, that he stands by helplessly while he allows tens of thousands of people to go to eternal damnation because of some ill-educated little radio preacher's doctrinal errors. Heresy comes in many forms, and surely one form is to place humanly devised limitations on the power and grace of God.

Why is it that we Christians seem to think so legalistically, so forensically, that we tend to spend far more time condemning and assigning blame than we do forgiving and extending grace? Does salvation come by grace through faith, or does it not? If it does, then surely we need to let go of some of the condemnation. Surely we need to commit others to the grace of God rather than demanding that they either see things our way or go to hell. Is there room for unity in our interpretive diversity, or must it always be "us against them"?

No wonder Christianity has so little to commend it in the eyes of the unbelieving public at the beginning of a new millennium. Christians are better known for their divisions and infighting, not to mention their relentless condemnation of "vile sinners," than for their love for one another. The Worldwide Church of God has learned that lesson the hard way. Only time will tell whether the lesson will stick or whether we will succumb to the temptation to find some new way to be God's "special and unique" people, a cut above the rest of the pack, the "faithful remnant."

The Hall of Administration on the Worldwide Church of God/Ambassador College campus in Pasadena, California. The Pasadena branch of Ambassador College consolidated in 1990 with its sister campus in Big Sandy, Texas, ending college operations in Pasadena. Ambassador University in Big Sandy closed in 1997.

Herbert W. and Loma Armstrong

Some of Herbert W. Armstrong's early evangelistic meeting flyers. Such personal public meetings were part of Armstrong's "Three-Point Campaign" launched in early 1934, consisting of the weekly half-hour radio program, the mimeographed Plain Truth *magazine for listeners, and personal evangelistic campaigns.*

THE PAIN OF CHANGE

WRITING ABOUT ORGANIZATIONAL CHANGE, Kenneth Gangel tells this poignant anecdote: "A professor once told his class that he would place on the board the most important principle relative to the process of change. Thereupon he turned and spent the next fifteen minutes etching out two words: GO SLOWLY."[1]

As a rule, we humans don't like change. By its very nature, change is accompanied by uncertainty, anxiety, and a certain amount of confusion, which naturally produce fear and reticence. Change is *always* met with resistance and often with open hostility.

By the grace of God, Herbert W. Armstrong's Worldwide Church of God was liberated from the bondage of self-absorbed sectarianism into a group of fellow citizens with God's people and members of God's household.[2] The transition, not surprisingly, was painful and difficult; the very identity of the church had to be changed.

CORE VALUES DECIMATED

All organizations have core values, even if they have never been committed to writing. They are the deeply and dearly held fundamental realities that make an organization what it is. An organization's core values shape how it treats people, makes decisions, weathers crises, plans for the future, and uses its resources. They are the blueprint for the organization's identity. Effective management of change, then, requires clear communication to all stakeholders (1) that the core values are *not* being changed, and (2) how the changes being made are consistent with and furthering the core values.

In the Worldwide Church of God, however, we found ourselves in the no-win situation of having to change the core values. The changes we were forced to make devastated the very sense of identity of our church and its members. Many thought their world was coming to an end. For the Worldwide Church of God, the normal organizational process was demolished at its source. With the dismantling and destruction of its core values, the Worldwide Church of God lost its vision and mission, which naturally set it sailing rudderless into a frustrating and confused void.

Before its changes, the Worldwide Church of God's core values included:

Doctrinal distinctives: These included the Sabbath, holy days, strict tithing, rejection of the doctrine of the Trinity, rejection of Christmas and Easter, observance of the Israelite clean and unclean meat laws, and belief that the destiny of humans is to become literal Gods in the God Family (God the Father and God the Son, both eternal and divine, and who created and rule the universe by the Holy Spirit, of which they are bodily composed and which is their power). They also included a definition of the gospel as precisely *not* about the person and saving work of Jesus Christ but rather as an announcement of the soon return of Christ and the establishment of the millennial kingdom as well as a warning message to the "lost ten tribes" (primarily the United States and Britain) about a rising "beast power" in Europe that will attack and punish them for their sins unless they repent. And certainly not least was the doctrine that the modern-day identity of the lost ten tribes is the key to understanding all Bible prophecy.

Founder distinctive: The special call and mission of Herbert Armstrong as God's one and only true end-time apostle raised up as the "Elijah to come" to "restore all things" before Jesus' return and to lead the faithful remnant of God's true church.

Identity distinctive: Members' own special status as the one and only true church. Members of the Worldwide Church of God were the only true Christians on earth because of their obedience to the "whole counsel of God" (especially the seventh-day Sabbath and the annual holy days) and to the command to preach the "true" gospel (see doctrinal distinctives above). For this obedience and their faithfulness in the face of a hostile "professing Christianity," they, along with the true saints (Sabbath-keepers, except for those who compete with the Worldwide Church of God), would be given immortality at Jesus' return (the first resurrection) and be the teachers of the masses in the millennial kingdom, instructing them in the law of God, especially regarding observance of the Sabbath and the holy days.

Mission distinctive: Use of mass media for mission as a fulfillment of end-time prophecy. The Worldwide Church of God believed that the prophecy of Jesus, "And this gospel of the kingdom shall be preached in all the world," could not be fulfilled until the invention of the printing press and the invention of radio. These instruments of mass communication, including television, were believed to have been given to humankind for the express purpose of Herbert Armstrong's using them to preach the gospel to the world. Armstrong's radio broadcast contracts in Europe and later in other continents were seen as the direct fulfillment of the prophecy that the true gospel would go into all the world. The proclamation of the gospel to the world was entirely on the shoulders of the Worldwide Church of God, since all the other churches were deceived and corrupt. It was thrilling for church members to see the gospel "going out in power" on television and radio and in nearly one hundred various booklets, magazines, books, and other publications.

One by one these core values shriveled and fell from the WCG tree. As they did, leaders and members became increasingly unsettled, fearful, and frustrated. "How are we different anymore?" "Where is all this leading?" "What will be changed next?" they asked.

The church these people had come into had slowly ceased to exist. The new church, for many, was nothing better than the particular Protestant churches they had left long ago. For many, bewilderment grew into anger, and anger into plans for forming their own church, a church that would respect and be faithful to the memory and teachings of Herbert Armstrong.

REAL CORE VALUES UNCOVERED

In the process of losing its distinctiveness and its *apparent* reason for being, however, I believe that the church uncovered its *true* core values. After all the extraneous doctrinal debris was scraped away, what remained was Jesus Christ. No need for uniqueness. No need to be special. No need for a special mission, a special message, a special leader, a special call. The only need was for the blood of the Lamb and the power of his resurrection. The *real* core values had been uncovered.

The true mission now seemed simple and plain—too simple and plain for most: Believe, live, and share the good news. But the reality is that the true vision of the Worldwide Church of God remains somewhat muddled. This is not surprising when one considers the journey this church has taken. Begun not as a church but as a media ministry, the church just "happened" in the wake of Armstrong's mass media proclamation. Until the day he died, Armstrong saw the role of the church as simply to stand behind him in prayer and financial support in his mission of preaching the gospel to the world. Today, without mass media, the church stands visionless, with a host of members still thinking of themselves, not as members of a local church, but as a group of special people called to support a powerful, globe-girdling media ministry.

Yet at the core of all church work must be the redemptive spirit. This is different from the spirit of desiring to do great things for God. It is a spirit of humility. It doesn't need to be noticed. It doesn't need to be seen to have powerful impact. It simply walks humbly with God. If church work is not redemptive, if it is not fragrant with pure gospel, if it does not resonate with the eternal harmonies of the grace of God in the face of Jesus Christ, then it is excess baggage.

THE SCOPE AND PACE OF CHANGE

It is important to distinguish between changing doctrine from a heretical position to that of historic Christianity on the one hand, and changing a doctrinal nuance within the context of historical Christianity or changing a policy, a procedure, or a cultural setting on the other. The first is nonnegotiable. It cannot be compromised. The other can be a matter for flexibility.

We made several mistakes in allowing matters of form, such as music styles and worship service times, to be placed on the change agenda rather than placing those issues on a much slower and more consensual track. We didn't see the professor's message on the chalkboard: GO SLOWLY.

When it came to doctrinal changes, however, we found ourselves having to weigh faithfulness to God and commitment to truth against sound principles of managing change. On the one hand, change was coming too fast to be assimilated. On the other hand, how could we sit on the truth? How could we deliberately allow our church to continue to believe and teach error and heresy? The responsibility to proceed with doctrinal changes once we became convicted of them was greater than the responsibility to go slowly. We came to see that there is a fundamental difference between making changes from heresy to truth and simply making changes from one way of doing things to another.

PARALYZED BY LEGALISM

Legalism chokes the love out of relationships. The truth of this came home to me one day when my teenage son pointed out to his mother and me: "Why can't you let me do things without telling me to? When you're always giving me orders, it takes all the pleasure out of it. I have to feel like I'm just following the orders instead of really caring about the family."

My son's problem was the church's problem. The love relationship was paralyzed because we never rose above just following orders. God wants a genuine love relationship with his beloved children, not an army of obedient robots. And he has, quite literally, gone to the greatest possible lengths to bring it about.

In the Worldwide Church of God, being free to love meant that we could redirect our energy from condemning society and sinners into proclamation of the message of God's love through Jesus Christ. It meant that we could declare the gospel instead of declaring lists of rules for right living and Republican party values statements. We could be *for* the gospel instead of merely being *against* sin and decadence. We could trust the Holy Spirit to bear fruit in the lives of those who hear the message instead of simply warning and walking away, waiting eagerly for the day when Jesus would return in glorious power to destroy all the rotten sinners.

These kinds of changes go far deeper than any changes in structure and technology. They are changes in core values, and they demand an entirely new perspective on who God is and who we are as well as on whom God loves and what God's real motives and goals are. Such changes proceed only from a heart transformed by the gospel.

In the Worldwide Church of God, we had the cart before the horse. To us, God would finally accept and save all those who proved themselves obedient and faithful. Our commitment was to what we believed to be the *way of life* that Jesus taught. We had to learn that our commitment needed to be to *Jesus himself*, not to a way of life. Only when we received *him* and his unlimited grace could we begin to walk in the new life of the kingdom of God—in the power of his resurrection, not in the power of our commitment.

This change is something that needs to involve each individual member of the church, not merely an organizational ideal or a doctrinal statement. And it can come about only in the face of the actual proclamation of the gospel, not merely in the face of changing doctrines.

In the Worldwide Church of God, stress was placed on "doing right things" in order to achieve godly character. Paul's analysis of the Jewish leadership was right on target in describing the Worldwide Church of God: "having a form of godliness, but denying its power" (2 Tim. 3:5). As Jack Hayford points out, "There is more to character formation than having learned a set of ideas—even if they are God's."[3] Because the Worldwide Church of God did not comprehend grace as the fountainhead of righteousness, the idea of formation of godly character was necessarily, though perhaps unwittingly, centered in outward conformity, not in inward transformation.

It is no exaggeration to say that if nothing else of a "productive" nature happens in the Worldwide Church of God[4]—even if the church organization fails, goes bankrupt, and disintegrates—the painful journey has already been infinitely successful. The most important thing that could ever have happened in the Worldwide Church of God has already taken place: Every person in the former Armstrong cult who truly wants to be set free in Christ now can be. Individual members have come to know for the first time the overwhelming power of the grace of God in Jesus Christ. No greater gift could have been given to this church and its members, and no greater blessing could have been received.

THE DILEMMA OF "APOSTOLIC AUTHORITY"

Adding to the pain of change in the Worldwide Church of God was the paradox of one pastor general contradicting another. In the Worldwide Church of God, the pastor general has absolute authority to set doctrine in the denomination. Whether it should be this way is another question, but the fact is that without such total authority, the changes in doctrine and direction would never have happened.

The span of control of the pastor general of the Worldwide Church of God extends to the entire organization. Herbert Armstrong, like most founders of organizations, had established the bylaws in such a way as to preserve his authority and control. He had the final word on doctrine, and members were comfortable with that. Members believed that God had placed Armstrong in his position and had given him the responsibility of establishing and maintaining doctrine, mission, and vision.

As Armstrong's personally chosen successor, Joseph Tkach Sr.'s authority lay not only in the constituted office of pastor general as dictated by the bylaws, but also in the trust the members had in Armstrong's choice, which they believed to be inspired of God. When Tkach began making changes in doctrines that had been established by Armstrong, personal loyalties were challenged on all fronts.

Yes, the pastor general has the authority and the responsibility to teach the truth, but Herbert Armstrong was "God's chosen apostle for the end time" who not only restored all truth to the church but also selected Tkach Sr. to succeed him. How could one "only true end-time apostle" contradict another "only true end-time apostle"? If one had restored the truth, how could another "unrestore" that same truth? Having placed one's faith in the credibility of Armstrong, even to the point of letting him define one's entire worldview and reason for existence itself, and now assuming he was wrong, how could one trust the credibility of Tkach Sr.? The question, How long before we find out that he is wrong, too? naturally began to cross members' minds.

Some members immediately accepted all changes simply because the changes came from Pasadena. They had decided long ago that they would be loyal to "God's government" in the church, and whatever Pasadena officially taught was fine with them. Of course, they had no basis for their acceptance of the changes other than blind faith that God was leading Pasadena. The obvious question, How can God, who is always faithful and true, lead Pasadena into error one day and into truth the next? did not seem to bother them.

Other members had been praying earnestly for the changes and welcomed them wholeheartedly. Still others carefully read and digested all explanations for the changes, giving themselves plenty of time and prayer, studying the biblical rationale, and keeping an open mind while they sought understanding from God. Most of these members came to see the errors in the previous teachings and embraced the new Worldwide Church of God, while a few remained convinced that the old doctrines were true.

At the other end of the spectrum were those who immediately and with hostility rejected anything new out of Pasadena as a satanic departure from the "faith once delivered" that God had given the church through Armstrong. As changes continued and it became more obvious that the church was moving farther from Armstrongism, the most vehement of these began aggressively undermining both headquarters and the changes. This resulted in predisposing many others against taking an unbiased look at either Armstrong's teachings or the changes.

The greatest number of members, however, seemed to be those who just wished the whole thing would go away. Some simply acted as if nothing had really changed. "This isn't really all that different from what we taught before," some reasoned. "I think it's mostly just a matter of semantics," was another easy perspective.

In the end, though, everybody had to finally accept the fact that monumental change had taken place in their church. The pastor general did have the authority to effect such change, and it had, in fact, been effected. In the Worldwide Church of God, the only level at which such essential change of core assumptions and values could have been brought about was at the level of pastor general. Attempts at any other level (there had been numerous short-lived attempts to change an Armstrong doctrine prior to Armstrong's death) would have simply resulted in those involved either recanting or being disfellowshiped.

Ironically, the same authoritarian governmental structure that created the heretical environment in the first place was necessary to correct it.

BARRIERS TO CONSENSUAL CHANGE ON DOCTRINE

Effective change management calls for broad involvement of people in the process. In this way, leaders can help as many people as possible at as many levels as possible develop a personal sense of "ownership" of the change.

When Joseph Tkach Sr. came to the point of realizing that the church must change its doctrine of the nature of God and accept the doctrine of the Trinity, the leadership team developed a process that we hoped would ensure a responsible and orderly introduction and implementation of the change. The first step was to bring together the headquarters leadership, regional pastors, and international regional directors for a careful presentation of the issues involved, demonstrating from an overview of basic theology the problems with our doctrine and the need to change it. Through this process we hoped to provide these leaders with the tools necessary for duplicating the process in their respective areas of responsibility and finally in the local congregations.

The goal was to involve senior and mid-level management in the process of doctrinal adjustment in such a way as to provide all necessary introduction and instruction, an opportunity for all questions to be thoroughly discussed and answered, and a collaborative development of a plan for implementation. The essential need for cooperation in regard to keeping the discussions confidential until we had reached consensus and all questions had been raised and answered was carefully stressed in the introductory session.

In spite of these efforts to seek a cooperative spirit that would minimize member confusion and ensure the greatest level of understanding and acceptance of the change as well as its most appropriate implementation, *by the end of the first day* of instruction and discussion, confidence had been widely broken and rumor, innuendo, and incomplete and erroneous information were telephoned, faxed, and e-mailed literally all around the world. The entire church was in an uproar before headquarters and regional leadership could even begin its second day of discussion on the topic of the triune nature of God.

I believe that several factors contributed to this predictable breakdown in our ability to manage the change of the doctrine of the Trinity in a consensual manner:

1. There was already widespread belief among pastors that a satanic conspiracy was at work among top leadership to destroy the church. The very fact that the conference was being held to discuss doctrine verified that belief.

2. For a cult to reject a false doctrine in order to embrace a core Christian doctrine is not a matter that can be handled by developing consensus. Consensus that the cult is wrong and traditional Christianity is right is impossible for cult members to achieve. Only an edict by the hierarchical government of the cult is capable of making such a change in the cult's doctrine. If the cult leadership attempts to wait until consensus can be achieved on a core doctrinal issue, the change will, necessarily, never happen.

3. Many, if not most, of the leaders who were opposed to any change in Herbert Armstrong's anti-Trinity doctrine had also been unable to accept Armstrong's appointment of Joseph Tkach Sr. as his successor. Any potential false move by Tkach provided political cannon fodder for their desire to see Tkach's leadership undermined or destroyed. The calling of the conference and its topic provided the ammunition they were looking for to convince their constituents that Tkach and the Pasadena gang were indeed destroying the church.

4. In the WCG corporate culture even a hint, a mere rumor of change in a core value sent shock waves through the organization. Even Herbert Armstrong deeply offended and alienated thousands of members by changing the day of observing Pentecost and the rules on remarriage after divorce. Since God has raised up Armstrong and given him the truth, many reasoned, even Armstrong himself had no right to change what God had revealed through him.

For these and likely more reasons, to try to develop consensus on such core values as the rejection of the Trinity or the Sabbath doctrine *before making the change* was by definition to sabotage the process before it began. Many, if not most, first-generation Sabbatarians are Sabbatarians because they *left* a non-Sabbatarian church, with all the resulting social and familial trauma, convinced after much study that the Sabbatarian position was correct. They had suffered for the truth, and God had honored their faithfulness.

To reject these doctrines now would be, in a very real sense, to declare that one had acted foolishly, not faithfully. It would be to abandon their sense of having done something special, something extraordinary for God. It would mean that they were not, after all, one of the only people who were not deceived. In fact, it would mean that they were actually among those who were even more deceived than others. Take, for example, this excerpt from an "open letter to the WCG" written by a "Seventh-Day Adventist scholar" and posted on the Internet:

> "Freedom of the Gospel." This interpretation of the freedom of the Gospel as freedom to pursue on the Sabbath one's personal pleasure and profit, rather than the presence and peace of God, can have disastrous consequences for the future of the WCG. It can weaken the commitment of your members to God and their church. Let me use an example to illustrate my point. Some time ago I was invited by the Seventh-day Baptist Church to speak in Rhode Island at a rally of about 50 of their pastors from the Eastern United States. As I listened to the pastors discussing some of their doctrinal beliefs, it soon became evident that there was a great diversity of beliefs and great freedom in interpreting the nature of the Gospel. Even the Sabbath was viewed by some more as a holiday than a holy day. When I asked them how did they feel about so much diversity in their church, one of them

replied: "This is what makes our Seventh-day Baptist church great. Members can believe and do what they like and still be members of the church."

Do doctrinal diversity and moral permissiveness really make a church great?[5]

Notice how this Sabbatarian author puts doctrinal diversity and moral permissiveness on the same level. Why does he do that? I don't know his heart, and I cannot presume to speak for him. But I do know why I used to do that, along with most Sabbatarian pastors I have known. To a strict Sabbatarian, doctrinal diversity *is* moral permissiveness. That is because doctrinal diversity suggests either that we, the Sabbatarians, might not have all the truth, or that God may not have nailed everything down as neatly as we had thought. That, in turn, means the Sabbath itself might be at risk of being undermined. And the prime directive of all Sabbatarians is to preserve the integrity of Sabbath observance at all costs.

Doctrinal changes that validate historical Christianity are by nature anathema to Sabbatarians. Historical Christianity is the corrupt evil empire that abolished Sabbath keeping in favor of the day of the ancient sun gods. To validate historical Christianity, then, is to lay an axe to the trunk of the Sabbatarian tree. If a Sabbatarian can find doctrinal corruption in the ancient church, then his Sabbath doctrine is reinforced. The more corrupt the ancient church, the less right it had to "abolish" the Sabbath. That is why some Sabbatarian groups tend to have anti-Trinitarian roots—not on the merits of the doctrine itself, but on the fear that if the ancient church were right about that, then there might be less chance that it was wrong about the Sabbath conclusions. (It was the Council of Nicea that ruled against Saturday as a day of worship, labeling it "Jewish," and ordered Sunday worship for all churches.)

Theoretically, doctrinal changes in the Worldwide Church of God would have been much smoother had there been greater pastor and member participation in their planning and implementation. This is only theoretical, however, because to involve pastors and members of a cult in the planning and implementation of doctrinal changes that completely transform the core assumptions and values of the cult is to destroy the process before it begins.

RESISTANCE AT ALL LEVELS

The doctrinal reforms of the Worldwide Church of God met with enormous resistance from every level of the organization. While many leaders and members had been praying for change and enthusiastically welcomed it, most were taken completely by surprise and were angered to find their church being "highjacked" and "dismantled" by the new leadership. In time, however, more began to respond to the gospel; and as they did, the need for the changes became clearer to them. As pastors and members embraced Jesus Christ as the ground and center of their lives, they had no more need for Herbert Armstrong or his "special mission."

Kenneth Gangel gives us a framework for the WCG story, citing seven dynamics that tend to accompany any kind of personal or organizational change. Each of these found expression in what happened in the Worldwide Church of God.

1. People will feel awkward, ill at ease, and self-conscious. Expect it. It's normal. I would go so far as to say that members of the Worldwide Church of God felt disoriented, lost, and stunned.

2. People initially focus on what they have to give up. Let them express it. It's a grieving process. Let it happen. We encouraged people to talk about how they felt. We affirmed their confusion and encouraged them to give themselves time to work through their feelings. We told them that their responses were normal and appropriate. This did not make the pain go away. It did not make the changes any easier, nor did it give us more credibility. Still, it was the right thing to do.

3. People feel alone, even if everybody is going through the same change. People tend to think others deal with things better than they do. It is important to remember that this natural sense of alone- ness during the crisis of change is a path of entry for the gospel. The insecurity and anxiety created by the disorientation of change means that the soul is naturally searching for the security and stability of its Maker.

4. People can handle only so much change. Know their tolerance levels. How much and how often. Magnitude and rapidity. These are factors that make change hard. Our backs were against the wall with this principle. When it comes to false doctrine, a church does not have the luxury of pacing the change. However, it is easy to confuse doctrine with administration, that is, to con- fuse substance with form. While we could not go slowly with the change of our doctrine on the nature of God, we should have gone much more slowly with changes in worship styles, for example.

5. People are at different levels of readiness for change. Therefore, their responses will vary significantly. How true this is. From the first change a decade ago and continuing to today, our members range from being enthusiastic about changes to being extremely angry about them, with every nuance in between. It is a constant challenge to effectively lead a group that finds itself in so many different spiritual, emotional, and philosophical places.

6. People will be concerned that they don't have enough resources. "I don't have what it takes." WCG members were frus- trated with their sense of powerlessness. Not only did they have no voice in the decision to change their cherished doctrines, but in a church culture that valued being able to understand and explain one's beliefs, they feared that they could not adequately understand the new doctrines.

7. If you take the pressure off, people will revert to their old behavior. People tend to hope the crisis will just go away. If we were to stop teaching the changes right now and invite members to go back to the old doctrines, I am convinced that a certain percentage would do so.[6]

PASTORAL RESISTANCE

Pastors who personally lacked the gospel—that is, who lacked the gospel *as the power of God for the salvation of all who believe*, as Paul describes it in the letter to the Romans—held back their congregations from growth in Christ. This factor was immensely frustrating and debilitating to those in the Worldwide Church of God who were hungry for a living church that loves Jesus, worships God, and lives and proclaims the gospel without reserve.

These pastors communicated to their congregations what I call "unjoy." That is the best word I can find to describe the distress, fear, embarrassment, dullness, and indifference they conveyed to their churches by their deliberate neutrality toward, if not avoidance of, all things truly Christian that touch the emotions, the heart, the soul, and the spirit. Many of these minority resister pastors were honest and upright men, wonderful fathers, good husbands and friends; but they were neither gifted nor equipped to lead a congregation of God's people to unfettered joy in the name of Jesus.

The excuses some of these pastors offered were plausible: "I don't want to drive away those who are having trouble with the changes. I want to be patient with them. I don't want them to feel unwelcome in their own church." These excuses sound loving and caring, and indeed, they may be born in part from a loving and caring heart. But the result is still the same: the gospel is not preached; and where the gospel is not preached, it does not penetrate.

A Crisis in Leadership

THE DOCTRINAL TRANSFORMATION OF the Worldwide Church of God left large numbers of its members confused, frustrated, worried, and angry. Members who were struggling with the upheaval in their church were in immediate and desperate need of one thing—*the gospel*.

They needed it every week in the sermon. They needed it in the music. They needed it in Bible studies. They needed it in pastoral counseling. They needed it in pastoral letters. They needed it in church socials and service projects. They needed it every time the pastor had the opportunity to share it, spread it, and shine it. But when a pastor didn't have it to spread, how could he spread it?

The most critical weakness in our journey of transformation was our shortage of pastors who were gospel-filled, unabashed lovers of Jesus Christ. This shortage of gifted, career pastors in the Worldwide Church of God is now being met in part as God calls bivocational pastors to lead our smaller congregations. These new leaders tend to have a fresh perspective on pastoral leadership. For the most part, they seem willing to learn new methods and are eager to equip others and share ministry. Above all, they seem to love Jesus Christ, love the gospel, love the people of God, and love teaching and spreading the Word.

The Worldwide Church of God was done great harm by pastors who were completely uncommitted to seeing the successful transformation of their congregations from old, Armstrong-style paradigms to a new, gospel-centered, gift-using, team-leadership-oriented church that loves Jesus and isn't afraid to live like it. Phillip Lewis says this: "Some people resist change more than others do because they feel more threatened."[1]

What did resistant WCG pastors have to lose? Limited accountability, "expert" status on doctrinal and biblical matters, authoritarian control, a perception of prestige and power, to name a few possibilities. We believe our current pastors have happily given these up, counting such things as loss that they might gain Christ. For some, this transition in pastoral priorities was nothing short of traumatic and painful. Others found such a transition personally impossible and left the Worldwide Church of God, claiming to believe they would be cut off from God if they ever "gave in" to the doctrinal transformation.

According to Kenneth Gangel, "Mature groups tend to change more quickly and more thoroughly than immature groups."[2] The fact that the Worldwide Church of God lost more than half of its pastors and members and more than 85 percent of its annual income during the course of its doctrinal changes indicates that it was a rather immature group. Its immaturity was reflected in its leadership as well as in its members. It has been solely by the grace of God that the church has fared as well as it has.

IMMEDIATE CHALLENGES

As the Worldwide Church of God faces an uncertain future, several significant factors demand attention.

1. *Critical shortage of called, gifted, Christ-centered, gospel-charged pastors.* Traditionally, pastors were selected from among graduates of the church's undergraduate college largely on the basis of their ability to defend the church's unique doctrines. The legalistic bent of the church put pastors firmly in a controlling mode. Today denominational leadership is committed to retraining its longtime pastors and placing new pastors only after

careful screening and training, including training and equipping in team-leadership styles of pastoral leadership.

2. *Member identity centered in national and global media ministry instead of in local church life and mission.* The movement that became the Worldwide Church of God began as Herbert Armstrong's media ministry. Listeners to his nationwide, and eventually worldwide, radio program became readers of his magazine and other literature. From among these, thousands became members of Armstrong's church. They were filled with a sense of mission: to support Armstrong's "God-given call" to preach the gospel in all the world through mass media and to warn the modern descendants of the lost ten tribes of Israel to repent and start keeping the seventh-day Sabbath. The motivation Armstrong provided them was his assurance that the faithful would be spared from the prophesied Great Tribulation and captivity at the hands of the united European beast power.

Today, members still tend to feel that "nothing is being done; the gospel is not being preached" unless church headquarters is deeply into mass media, especially television or radio. Our challenge as denominational headquarters is to lead local congregations, through their pastoral leadership, into a fresh sense of God's unique vision for them as a local reality of the body of Christ.

3. *Friends and family members in Armstrong-preserving splinter groups.* It is stressful for members to have friends and family members who have broken off fellowship to form or join splinter groups that strongly oppose the doctrinal changes in the Worldwide Church of God. This creates a long-term strain on the reasons for remaining in any given church fellowship, including the Worldwide Church of God. Our challenge is to seek God's will for the Worldwide Church of God and to communicate his will effectively to the members. Why do we exist and what is our unique contribution to the kingdom of God? These are questions to which WCG members need God's answers.

4. *Members in various stages of grief and anger from Armstrongism and confusion about Herbert Armstrong's role in their*

lives. Even members who understand intellectually the errors of Armstrong's doctrines and have accepted historic Christianity still have to emotionally work through their ties to Armstrong's intensely charismatic and grandfatherly impact on their lives. We are committed to the proclamation of the gospel to our members so that they can find true freedom from past destructive paradigms and emotional entanglements.

5. *Continuing member distrust of denomination headquarters brought on in part by decades of failed prophecies, former leadership extravagance, and recent sweeping doctrinal changes.* Although it is the current administration that is humanly responsible for the end of legalism, extravagance, and doctrinal error, members tend to place the blame for the past problems on a nondescript concept of "headquarters." In the past, the legalistic environment and the belief that the Worldwide Church of God was the "only true church" caused members to bury most of their dissatisfaction. Today, the long-buried anger is coming out, and much of it is directed toward headquarters. Our challenge is to be attentive to the needs of church members and respond to them in loving patience with the healing balm of the gospel of grace.

6. *General sense of frustration and loss of identity due to dramatic decreases in membership and income resulting in elimination of television programming, free literature distribution, and numerous church programs and in the closing of the church university, grade school, and high school.* Our challenge is to help our members see beyond the outward appearance of numbers, reputation, and prestige to the true power and joy of the humble life hidden in Christ.

7. *Increasing globalization and a rapidly changing world that the church does not understand and has not equipped itself to serve.* We are working to encourage a sense of local mission and vision in each of our congregations, primarily through pastoral training that is sensitive to, and responsive to, the movement of the Holy Spirit in meeting the changing needs of today's troubled society.

8. *Members who are shackled by legalism and don't know, or if they do know, aren't yet able to feel, that they are accepted and loved*

by God. We are committed to a multilevel proclamation of the gospel to our members through printed and electronic church publications, pastoral training, regional celebrations, and evangelistic preaching. We are also committed to helping each congregation in the development of spiritually healthy small groups in which members can be nurtured in the context of active and caring body life in the power and love of Jesus Christ.

9. *Members divided and factious over doctrinal changes and their implications.* Even though some time has passed, some members still hold the doctrines of Armstrong and are praying for and waiting for the time when "God will clean the liberals out of headquarters and put things back on track." We are committed to unceasing prayer for these people and for constant passionate proclamation of the gospel to them.

10. *Fear of openness or honesty in relationships due to the church's history of judgmentalism, gossip, and broken confidences.* Although much progress has been made in instituting small groups, many members still are very uncomfortable opening up to other members in our fellowship. The history of legalism makes it difficult to trust others. At denominational headquarters, we are committed to modeling trustworthy and dependable leadership under the lordship of Christ so that in time an atmosphere of genuine trust and credibility can prevail in the Worldwide Church of God. The mountain to climb to restore a general sense of trust and credibility in our fellowship is of greater proportions than Everest. Yet with God all things are possible. A major key will be our success in creating a new kind of relationship between denominational headquarters and local pastors and members.

Chip Bell asks:

> How do you get passion without promise [of tangible benefits]? Devotion without dividends? The secret may lie in creating an environment in which leaders treat followers more like partners than underlings.

The new "partner-leader" focuses less on sovereignty and more on support. Controlling takes a back seat to coaching.[3]

We are attempting to turn denominational headquarters into a service and resource center that exists to help each congregation be all it can be in Christ. We believe that only by serving, rather than by ruling, does our denominational headquarters, and indeed, do our churches as a worldwide denomination, have a viable and productive future.

CORPORATE SELF-PERPETUATION VS. GENUINE RENEWAL

A challenge for the Worldwide Church of God is, and will continue to be, to allow renewal to be more than a cosmetic change in outward doctrine and to resist exchanging one brand of authoritarianism for another. To be genuine, the renewal must be a renewal of individual hearts, an awakening or a reawakening of the call to each member of the church to become all that God has created him or her to be. The church as a corporate entity—that is, as a body—must see itself fundamentally as a tool that exists to create the sort of atmosphere or climate in which every member is, in fact, able to reach his or her potential as an individual who is vital to the health and effectiveness of the whole body.

The lure for the church corporation to adopt a maintenance orientation as over against a service orientation is strong and is most likely the natural tendency of things in this broken world, but it must be resisted with an unrelenting commitment to the gospel in all its sacrificial implications. It is, after all (as Rom. 1:16 affirms) the *gospel* that is "the power of God for the salvation of everyone who believes." The corporation of the church must let the gospel have its way, all the way. Self-perpetuation is the opposite of the self-giving principle inherent in the life, death, and resurrection of the Son of God for the salvation of human beings. For the church politic to survive, it must exist to *give away* ministry, not to maintain its own integrity.

Tex Sample writes in *U.S. Lifestyles and Mainline Christian Churches* that each church must come to understand itself—its own identity, style, program, and image—and then serve the people God has prepared it to serve in the ways God has equipped it to serve. The Holy Spirit is already loose in the world, Sample points out, which means that no matter where we go with the gospel, Christ is already there preparing the way.[4]

In the Worldwide Church of God, we have seen that we need a new identity, style, program, and image—ones that spring from the collective Spirit-given power of individual hearts transformed by, and passionate for, the gospel of the Son of God. That leads us to make our first priority the unflagging proclamation of that gospel to all members who remain with us. Christ is and has been already at work among our members, preparing the way. Far above mere changes of doctrinal statements, our task continues to be one of unceasing prayer and proclamation to the end that every member in our fellowship might come to know and live in the fullness of the grace of God.

THE CREDIBILITY FACTOR

Kenneth Gangel points out that the credibility of any ministry depends on the credibility of its leaders.[5] When people can't trust their leaders, they will not follow them with their hearts. Then the only thing left is raw expediency: I will follow only as long as I am benefited.

As I said earlier, the Worldwide Church of God is experiencing a crisis of leadership credibility. The effect of massive changes and our paralysis caused by the laborious process of selling the 50-acre headquarters facility have created a sense of frustration on both sides of the doctrinal changes. Those who yearn to "move forward" as a church are frustrated because they do not have the financial resources they believe they need. Conversely, those who want to see the church return to Armstrongism are frustrated because they do not see that happening.

Not only is credibility flagging, but raw expediency is also wearing thin. Benefits have become fewer and fewer. Members with children are looking at larger churches where more programs and opportunities are offered for youngsters. Members who are weary of meeting on Saturday and listening to announcements about Old Testament festivals are looking elsewhere for a church home that isn't weighed down with Sabbatarian paradigms.

"Why doesn't Pasadena do something?" is a sentiment felt in many quarters. Yet there is wide disagreement on just what Pasadena should do. Some believe it should abandon Saturday and the annual festivals entirely, thereby alienating once and for all the traditionalists, many of whom are the people whose sacrifice and commitment built and sustained the church for decades. Some believe Pasadena should continue to affirm both the Old Testament religion and the new covenant in Christ in an effort to keep traditionalists attending until the gospel takes root in their hearts. If that course is maintained, opponents argue, then within another five years, the only people who will be left in the church will be the traditionalists.[6]

Some pastors have urged that the headquarters structure be dismantled so that the congregations can make their own way as independent churches. This option seems irresponsible because it would surely result in the collapse of scores of congregations. Denominational headquarters is, in fact, entrusted with the custodianship of the worldwide fellowship of its congregations. Its decisions and planning must therefore be geared toward the healthy spiritual and structural preservation of the worldwide entity, that is, the continued viability, connectivity, and integrity of the Worldwide Church of God as an international body.

Trust, of course, is a two-way street. Robert Greenleaf says that great leaders, regardless of their gruff exteriors, have "empathy and an unqualified acceptance of the persons of those who go with their leadership."[7] I pray that is true of me and the other WCG leaders. Greenleaf observes, "Acceptance of the person, though, requires a tolerance of imperfection. Anybody could lead perfect people—if there were any."[8] Praise God for his grace!

Although we may sometimes feel as weary as Moses must have felt with the Israelites, Robert Greenleaf is surely right when he says, "It is part of the enigma of human nature that the 'typical' person—immature, stumbling, inept, lazy—is capable of great dedication and heroism *if* wisely led."[9] The Holy Spirit leads us in perfect wisdom; in our brokenness, we have a problem passing it down. Yet in the end, the Spirit is the true leader of administrators, pastors, and members alike.

Our current financial challenges and generally flagging morale may finally prove irreversible. Some of this is the result of the issues I mention in this book, but much of it reflects the challenges facing denominations in general in the United States. At WCG headquarters, our first priority will continue to be to see to it that every congregation has a competent, Christ-centered, and Spirit-led pastor, because we believe that the key to congregational success lies in pastoral leadership. Yet whatever the future may hold for our church organization, by the infinite power and grace of God we can say with all joy and peace of heart, "It is well with my soul." We have already received the greatest gift imaginable.

Ambassador Auditorium, the centerpiece of the headquarters campus of the Worldwide Church of God in Pasadena, California. The auditorium was renowned for its world-class concert series that ran from 1974 to 1995.

THE PATH OF RENEWAL

IN EARLY 1995 A large group of pastors opposed to change sent three representatives to Pasadena to discuss a compromise. They proposed allowing two kinds of churches and pastors in the Worldwide Church of God: (1) those who accept and teach the new doctrines, and (2) those who believe and teach traditional Armstrong doctrines. When this proposal was rejected as an affront to the gospel, the ministers defected, taking several thousand members with them.

I remember a conversation with one close pastor friend who could not understand why we were "destroying everything God built through Herbert Armstrong." After we had proceeded through passage after passage demonstrating the error of Armstrong's doctrines, he finally threw up his hands in frustration and said, "But Mike, what do you do with the fact that God revealed all these doctrines to Mr. Armstrong? We can't throw out his inspiration. God showed him how to interpret the Bible on these things correctly, and that's why we're not deceived like the other churches."

"But if he was wrong about these things, then God *didn't* reveal them," I tried to explain.

"Well, I just don't see it that way. I think God revealed these things to Mr. Armstrong, and you guys are just rejecting that inspiration. And I'll tell you, there are a lot of us who think so."

Since reformation in the Worldwide Church of God began among members of its highest leadership, those leaders who were not being moved by the Spirit toward change began to take on the role of what Howard Snyder calls "keepers of the institution."[1] For them, the survival of the church itself, as founded and fashioned by Herbert Armstrong, was at stake. Consequently, the institutional leaders who opposed the movement toward reformation brought steady pressure to bear on the pastor general, at first attempting to convince him to dispose of the leaders who supported the renewal, and finally by organizing themselves to lead the church membership into a new church that would preserve the Armstrong doctrines and traditions.

Because WCG governance did not allow the removal of the pastor general, the vitality of the renewal movement lay in the vitality of the pastor general to keep it on track. Had Joseph Tkach Sr. not kept up the pressure for reform, the movement would have stalled. It would simply have been swallowed up in sixty years of tradition and institutionalization, as had earlier efforts that did not have the backing of Herbert Armstrong.

KEY ELEMENTS OF RENEWAL

As I reflect on what I consider to be key elements of the transformation of the Worldwide Church of God, I am indebted to Howard Snyder's study of Pietism, Methodism, and Moravianism in which he distills a number of features common to the process of corporate spiritual renewal in those movements.[2] Although the process documented by Snyder bears remarkable similarities to what happened in the Worldwide Church of God, for the most part the WCG journey was unique. I believe this is the case, in large part, because the original formation of Armstrong's church was itself a reaction to the supposed "deadness" of modern Christianity.

Herbert Armstrong and all true believers in Armstrongism saw the history of the Christian church as nothing other than a grand conspiracy. Armstrong declared:

Jesus proclaimed the Gospel of the KINGDOM OF GOD—which is the GOOD NEWS of the WORLD

TOMORROW! Soon men went out proclaiming CHRIST—they appropriated *His Name* and the prestige of *His Name* in order to *deceive* the world, and to HIDE from the world the MESSAGE that CHRIST brought. But, in this *end*-time, when the *end* of this age is at hand, *this same Gospel of the Kingdom of God*—the GOVERNMENT of God—being born into the *family* of God—this *same* Gospel is *now* once again going to ALL THE WORLD! *That* prophecy is being fulfilled in "*The* WORLD TOMOR-ROW" broadcast and in the pages of *The* PLAIN TRUTH![3]

Convinced that he was a lone, courageous "voice crying out in the wilderness of religious confusion," Armstrong saw himself and his church as the specially called end-time revival of God's faithful remnant people. Consequently, any call to renewal among the followers of Armstrong that moved toward historic Christianity was naturally viewed as a "return to Babylon" and was strongly opposed.

For adherents of Armstrongism, the only kind of renewal that makes sense is one that constitutes a return to the "faith once delivered," or the so-called original purity of the church, meaning behaviors rooted in the "traditions of the fathers" that characterized the Jewish Christianity of the early Jerusalem church.

Since Armstrong's church believed it had already captured the purity of the first-century church, the idea of its need to return to the primitive faith tended to be incomprehensible for WCG members. The *other* churches had become "Christians in name only," not us.

Armstrong's desire for renewal in the larger body of Christ was certainly justifiable. However, his solution was no solution, but rather a worsening of the problem, leading Christians, not closer to the power of the gospel, but farther away from it. Consequently, the Worldwide Church of God found itself approaching the question from the other ditch, having once rejected the "broken" mainstream Christian church and now, in the throes of renewal, having to reembrace its validity.

A rocky process to say the least, the renewal of the World-wide Church of God has caused no less than three major splits (to date). History will have to judge the strengths and deficiencies of its spiritual transformation, but all things considered, I believe eight key elements[4] emerge as fundamental characteristics of the WCG renewal.

Key 1: Rediscovery of the Triune God and the Person of the Holy Spirit

Herbert Armstrong's church began with a strong emphasis on the Word without a corresponding emphasis on the Spirit. Due in part to his early experiences with members of a neighboring Pentecostal church, Armstrong strongly distrusted and vehemently opposed the entire Pentecostal movement, calling it "the devil's counterfeit."[5] The result of Armstrong's intense overreaction to all things remotely Pentecostal[6] was the formation of a highly legalistic sect.

The WCG renewal was bathed in a rediscovery of the doctrine of the Trinity, especially the concept of the personhood of the Holy Spirit. The renewal movement in the Worldwide Church of God remained firmly committed to Armstrong's ideal of faithfulness to Scripture but welcomed a place for the movement and fellowship of the Spirit. This significant course correction led the church onto fertile ground for the blossoming of the gospel in the hearts of WCG members.

Key 2: Rediscovery of the Gospel

A new perception of the faith lay at the heart of the reformation of the Worldwide Church of God. From my own perspective as executive assistant to the church's pastor general, the fundamental issue became the question "What is a Christian?"

In 1987, while teaching an undergraduate class on the General Epistles at Ambassador College in Pasadena, I was confronted with the bare declaration of 1 John 5:1: "Everyone who believes that Jesus is the Christ is born of God, and everyone who loves the father loves his child as well." If that statement is true, that *everyone* who believes that Jesus is the Christ is born of God, then a person clearly does not have to be a Sabbatarian to be saved. I knew of many people who were not Sabbatarians but who believed that Jesus is the Christ, and that belief had most definitely transformed their lives.

In the Worldwide Church of God, however, we would quickly say, "Well, you had better read verses 2 and 3: "This is how we know that we love the children of God: by loving God and carrying out his commands. This is love for God: to obey his commands. And his commands are not burdensome." Then we would argue that the commands of God include the Saturday Sabbath; therefore, if you don't keep the Saturday Sabbath, then you do not love God.

I fell for that argument for nearly forty years, thinking I was standing faithfully with God and not realizing I was in fact standing in condemnation of all believers who didn't keep the Sabbath. Our mindset prevented us from taking seriously the *next* two verses: "For everyone born of God overcomes the world. This is the victory that has overcome the world, even our faith. Who is it that overcomes the world? Only he who believes that Jesus is the Son of God" (1 John 5:4–5).

The commands to which John is referring are *not* the commands of the old covenant. They are the commands he has already mentioned numerous times in his letter, specifically: "And this is his command: to believe in the name of his Son, Jesus Christ, and to love one another as he commanded us. Those who obey his commands live in him, and he in them" (1 John 3:23–24). The ironic truth is that our exclusion of fellow believers on the basis of non–Sabbath keeping was to break the very commands John was proclaiming. We did not accept the truth that salvation comes by faith in the name of Jesus (for us it was

Jesus plus Sabbath), and it is not love to call fellow Christians "deceived children of the devil."

Pastor general Tkach Sr. and I discussed these issues often. How to understand and what to do about the plain truth that was becoming increasingly clear to us was a painful and rocky process. We were coming from full immersion in Armstrongism, fighting not only a concrete-encased corporate identity and a tradition etched in stone but also our own personal sense of identity, purpose, and call.

Key 3: From the Top Down

The renewal movement in the Worldwide Church of God was centered in its own hierarchy. As a result, denominational resources were all directed toward insuring the success of the reforms, including recorded sermons and special presentations required to be played in all congregations, the pastor general's monthly letter to all members and regular financial supporters, his monthly newsletter to pastors, the membership-wide monthly church newspaper, and all other church publications. Renewal leaders serving close to Tkach Sr. were raised to the church's highest ecclesiastical rank, giving additional credibility to their roles in the renewal efforts; and their sermons and articles were officially distributed in all WCG congregations.

Despite the clear advantage of the renewal movement originating in the denomination's highest leadership, however, local pastoral leadership proved to be an essential key to the effectiveness of the renewal at the local level. Pastors who were committed to Armstrongism saw the reforms as a threat to the church's identity as the "one and only" true church and saw it as their duty to oppose them. Perhaps that is the inevitable result when one of the fundamental aspects of the renewal itself is a redefinition of the identity of the existing body and a renouncing of major doctrinal errors, upon many of which the church itself was founded.

Doctrinal change in Armstrong's church could only come "from the top down." By God's grace, the renewal nucleus included the president and enough significant leaders to insure the success of the decision-making process and communication to church members. As Armstrong's successor, Joseph Tkach Sr. held the same church authority as had Armstrong. Members looked solely to him as the basis of authority, under Christ and in accord with Scripture, for church doctrine, vision, and mission.

Because Tkach Sr. did not possess the same facility of written and oral expression as Armstrong, he had to rely heavily on others for his written communication to pastors and church members. The tiny headquarters renewal cell consisting of Tkach Sr. and me, his executive assistant and editorial advisor, was soon joined by Greg R. Albrecht, then church booklet editor, and soon thereafter by Joseph Tkach Jr., then executive director of pastors. As time progressed, other headquarters leaders began to provide a certain degree of conceptual support as they "bought into" the need for certain changes or in some cases had long seen the need for them.

Slowly, despite major opposition from those headquarters leaders who found the new direction appalling and dangerous, the new paradigms being promoted in church literature began to find fertile soil in increasing numbers of church members and pastors, and informal small group cells (both for and against the new ideas) began to emerge in response.

Soon we discovered that not only was the Holy Spirit at work among the Pasadena hierarchy, but his redemptive touch was being felt around the world. Members and pastors alike began to write to let us know that they had recently been confronted with the simplicity and power of the gospel and therefore with major deficiencies in WCG theology, and that they were in prayerful distress about what action to take when this or that article or letter from the pastor general would arrive announcing a particular change in church doctrine or practice. It became increasingly clear that the Holy Spirit was at work throughout the church worldwide, with the headquarters leadership renewal being simply one part, however necessary, of the Lord's program for denomination-wide renewal.

The gospel broke into our hearts like a clear, fresh, bubbling mountain brook after an exhausting, seemingly endless climb over burning rocks and parched soil on a blistering day. It was everything our souls craved and longed for. It was the power of God for salvation bursting upon us like the light of day and like shouts of rescue to hopeless souls, beaten, starved, and imprisoned in darkness. *God accepts sinners!* It was scandalous. It was impossible. Or was it? Isn't that what our use-worn Bibles had said all along? But to actually believe it, and to believe it could be true *of me* was to move from merely knowing *about* Jesus to begin to know *him!*

Key 4: Emergence of Small Groups

One of the first effects of a rediscovery of the gospel in the Worldwide Church of God was a hunger for purposeful fellowship among those who were tasting or retasting the joy and freedom of salvation in Jesus Christ. Church headquarters conducted pastoral seminars on small groups and made instructional videotapes on small groups available on a loan basis to all pastors. In congregations where pastors were enthusiastic about a renewed sense of worship and spiritual fellowship, many members responded enthusiastically to the opportunity to be involved in a new and more intimate form of body life. A WCG values brochure, *Vision 2000*, contains this statement about small group worship:

> Every Christian is called into active fellowship with the Body of Christ. Personal spiritual growth takes place not in a large gathering, but in the context of small group life. We encourage participation, in a non-threatening setting at one's own comfort level, in small group worship. Such

small group worship settings provide opportunity to get to know other Christians, to worship and praise God, discuss questions, study the Bible, share concerns, pray and receive prayer in a non-judgmental environment. Small groups form the core of congregational life, and are an ideal way for guests and visitors to become familiar with Christian faith and practice in a comfortable, supportive and pressure-free setting.[7]

The tension created in local congregations by the changes in doctrine and vision of church headquarters proved a formidable challenge for church members. "Are you with headquarters or against headquarters?" Those who were "with" headquarters spiritually tended to find themselves coming together in small groups for prayer and worship as they experienced a renewed love for the Word of God. Those who were "against" headquarters, but who joined a small group and remained in it, tended to find themselves becoming more comfortable with the changes in their church.

Most congregations have within them at least one strong small group fellowship in which participants are committed to one another in terms of mutual spiritual support, prayer, and worship. In many instances, a thriving small group has positively influenced the larger congregation. Throughout the church, such groups have promoted the spiritual vitality and general well-being of the denomination as a whole, demonstrating that new life is indeed springing up in the midst of what might otherwise have remained a stale and moribund spiritual environment.

Key 5: Rediscovery of the Priesthood of Believers

The priesthood of believers is a concept that has only recently become part of the vocabulary of the Worldwide Church of God. Historically, the 65-year-old church invested all of its evangelistic energy into the media work of church headquarters and all of its pastoral work in its professional pastors.

The nonordained members were expected to "pray and pay" and live godly, upright lives. Ministry opportunities for members were limited to serving the needs of other members, and in most congregations these opportunities were handed out by pastors.

Greg Ogden, author of *The New Reformation*, points out that the New Testament does not limit ministry to the ordained clergy: "Nowhere does the term 'ministry' or 'minister' refer to a particular class of people set apart from the rest of the church. The noun *diakonia* is variously translated 'service,' 'ministry,' or 'mission.' The personal form of the noun *diakonos* is translated 'servants,' 'ministers,' or 'deacons,' depending on its context."[8] Ogden sees the ordained clergy as having the function of "helping the members of the body discover their ministry to upbuild the church and be deployed to the world."[9] In this way the entire body of Christ can participate in its call to be one in which "each part is working properly" and in which each part "promotes the body's growth in building itself up in love" (Eph. 4:16, NRSV).

Martin Luther taught that the housemaid scrubbing on her knees is doing a work as pleasing to God as the priest on his knees before the altar. In other words, since we are all here for God's purpose and not our own, we are, in effect, his emissaries on his mission in whatever particular situation we might be. In that light, it is easy to see that every member of the body of Christ is indeed specially called and placed into ministry, and that one is not greater or lesser than another.

The New Reformation is assigned reading for all WCG pastors and has been of great help in encouraging a fresh perspective on the priesthood of believers in our fellowship. Since 1995 the church has seen significant increase in personal ministries of all kinds, including a strong and growing emphasis on leadership development among women and teens.

The Worldwide Church of God has learned by hard experience that loudly condemning sinful practices and telling people how to live doesn't lead them to their Savior. Instead, the church must let itself be the loving hands and arms of Jesus at work in the world. The priesthood of believers must be a reality that is lived out, by the power of the Holy Spirit, in the everyday life of the church, of congregations, of small groups, of families, of individual Christians. Jesus calls all his people into his kingdom, and every subject of his kingdom has an essential role to play in the kingdom of the one who heals, restores, blesses, and gives.

Key 6: Growing Sense of Identification with the Universal Church

One of the first results of the renewal of the Worldwide Church of God was a sense of belonging to the universal body of Christ. The joy of this fresh awakening to a place in the family of God generated among renewed church leaders and members a passion for breaking down the walls of denominationalism.

Invitations to address our members were extended to leaders of other denominations. Non–WCG Christian educators were invited to conduct training seminars with WCG pastors. WCG leaders and members began visiting other churches, establishing friendships and professional relationships with members of other Christian churches. WCG congregations began sharing facilities with congregations of other denominations, and WCG pastors began joining ministerial alliances and seeking opportunities for partnership and cooperation with other churches. And the magazine Herbert Armstrong founded, *The Plain Truth*, completely revised its editorial policies to become an interdenominational magazine committed to promoting understanding, unity, and partnership between Christians of all denominations.

Key 7: Rediscovery of Outreach

A reaching beyond the boundaries of our fellowship was one of the first results of the renewal process. We suddenly felt the need to let down the drawbridge and drain the moat. As early as 1986, Joseph Tkach Sr. began to encourage members to become an active part of their communities, to make friends outside the church, and to join community associations and clubs. "How can we be salt and light to the world around us if we stay hidden away in our holy little caves?" Tkach reasoned.

The new emphasis on making friends "in the world" and actively ministering the grace of God to the unsaved was a dramatic turnaround from the cloistered premillennial dispensational mindset that had prevailed under Armstrong's leadership. Nevertheless, the "coming out" is slow to take hold. The fact that all the members of the church are called to become fully the unified ministering agents of Christ in the world has profound implications both for what we call "the laity" and for what we call "the ministry." In every case of God's call, the person or community is called for God's larger redemptive purpose, not merely for the sake or benefit of those called. The same applies to the church today. Not only is the church called for the sake of the world, but every member in the church has a vital and God-given role to play in that mission.

The church exists for the world, not merely for itself. The beauty of this biblical truth influences the very reason for being of the church and indicts the fortress mentality that reigned supreme in the Worldwide Church of God. Interaction with the "world"—that is, with people who were not members of the Worldwide Church of God—was discouraged. Proclamation and mission were restricted to the mass media work of denominational headquarters, meaning that members (not to mention local pastors) were effectively excluded from any sense of mission.

Members were encouraged to spend most of their discretionary time with each other, eschewing unnecessary contact with the world. Home schooling, home births, avoidance of all non-emergency medical care, and avoidance of community sports and recreation programs were a few of the effects of the exclusivist mentality that pervaded the church. The net effect of this inwardness, this pursuit of a pious and righteous safe haven behind the comfortable walls of a nonthreatening church network, was a fundamental fear and distrust of all things non–Worldwide Church of

God, and worse, a profound failure to participate in the Spirit-led mission life of the body of Christ.

Herbert Armstrong's sense of his own divine call to fulfill the "end-time Elijah work" of preparing the way for Christ's second coming set him and his church at odds with all other Christian churches and added to, rather than diminished, the confusion and division in the body of Christ that Armstrong was so quick to condemn in others. Over the past decade, the Holy Spirit has moved us away from ourselves and toward Jesus, resulting in the refreshing recognition that we are not the sum total of the body of Christ.

Key 8: Redefinition of the Mission of the Church

Correction of the erroneous doctrines of Herbert Armstrong required a corresponding correction of the church's mission. Because our sense of identity had been so wrapped up in Armstrong's mass media "end-time warning witness," the general mission of "simply spreading the gospel in word and deed like all the other churches" seemed so broad as to be meaningless to many. Without a specific and clearly articulated denominational sense of mission that was on par with the former one, many pastors and members were left feeling purposeless. "What are we doing?" "Why do we exist?" "What is happening?" With the focus shifted from national and international mass media to relational evangelism at the local and personal level, many were lost and bewildered.

Feeling rudderless, many people simply looked elsewhere for a sense of meaning. For some "all this Jesus stuff" was sheer nonsense anyway, and they formed splits to preserve Armstrongism, which they perceived as the "faith once delivered to the saints." Others, exhausted by the whole experience, simply dropped out of organized religion. A few began to flaunt their newfound freedom in Christ as a license to irritate others or to sin freely. However, others, feeling released to worship without the bonds of

Armstrongism, formed new worship groups and ministries within the Worldwide Church of God or began attending other Christian churches.

For the moment, after all the church has been through, it could be argued that its specific mission is to rest in Christ's arms for healing and survival. At some point, however, a clear and dynamic sense of denominational mission will have to emerge. Aubrey Malphurs has written that a church or ministry without a God-given, clearly articulated and implemented vision will neither thrive nor long survive.[10] The Worldwide Church of God is currently struggling with this impediment. Since the death of Herbert Armstrong and subsequent repudiation of his vision and mission, the denomination has found no replacement compelling enough to capture the hearts and imagination of members.

The denomination has, of course, a general sense of the call to proclaim the gospel in all the world, to train and commission pastors, and to nurture its local congregations in the faith. But a clear and focused vision for the Worldwide Church of God as a unique entity within the context of the universal body of Christ is vague at best. The void has led to a certain degree of confusion, with various unrefined and undeveloped points of view emerging—both in leadership and in the rank and file—and vying for supremacy.

It may be that the Worldwide Church of God is not quite ready for a compelling vision. It may be that the fellowship needs sufficient time for healing and reflection before conditions are right for God to begin to share what his plan is for a church that is currently still in shock. It may be, then, that the church is moving appropriately through a process that God has in mind, with a vision still in early fetal stages and steadily being cultivated by the Holy Spirit to be made clear and compelling in God's perfect time.

I believe the right vision will emerge for the Worldwide Church of God as we continue to place ourselves before God for his purposes to be fulfilled through our church. If that is true, then the best and most productive years of the church lie yet ahead.

THE JOURNEY CONTINUES

There is simply no such thing as a one-size-fits-all program for negotiating the treacherous waters of renewal. In the Worldwide Church of God we are often lauded and praised for our journey from legalism into the freedom of grace in Christ. Yet I often remind myself and others that our journey is not over, that we have not arrived at the destination, that we have not suddenly become a church completely free of legalism, faithlessness, and heresy. Jesus has set us on the path, and the Holy Spirit is moving us down that path. But the journey is that of a lifetime.

The painful reality of a changing church is that not all members stand together during the process. The Worldwide Church of God has experienced a profound change in identity and mission, including the profound paradigmatic change from a one-man-dominated ministry to the ministry of all believers. The pain has been enormous, resulting in the exodus of more than half of the church's members and clergy, and denominational leaders have had to find superhuman power in Christ for perseverance and patience. Yet the Spirit-implanted vision for the needed change has, by God's grace, carried us through. As I have said before, an ironic dynamic is that change of such magnitude virtually demands a hierarchical, authoritative form of church government, even though a necessary aim of the mountain of change is the demise of such a form of government.

STRATEGIES FOR
SOUND BODY LIFE

I HAVE NO QUESTION that the single most important God-given blessing that led to the transformation of the Worldwide Church of God was the church's unqualified belief that the Bible is the inspired Word of God and that as such it is at all times the final authority on all matters of doctrine, faith, and practice. Despite Herbert Armstrong's destructive belief that he was the sole end-time interpreter of Scripture, his firm teaching that the Bible must, in the final analysis, carry the day was God's implanted gift to the fellowship Armstrong founded. Within weeks of the death of Herbert Armstrong, that implanted essential truth began to break the soil and reach sunward in the Worldwide Church of God, as I have discussed in the first chapter.

The writer of Hebrews said, "Indeed, the word of God is living and active, sharper than any two-edged sword, piercing until it divides soul from spirit, joints from marrow; it is able to judge the thoughts and intentions of the heart" (Heb. 4:12, NRSV). This wonderful truth did us no good as long as we turned a blind eye to the fact that it was for us. Not merely for others, but for *us*.

For the Worldwide Church of God, the Word of God had become a holy tool to demonstrate our superior obedience. It had become a righteous club to hold over the heads of others to keep them under control. But the Word of God is not ours to use as we please. It is the guiding light of truth that exposes our own failure and shame, and our own crying need for God's love and grace.

Even though we were fully committed to the Word of God, we understood much of it through the lens of Herbert Armstrong's interpretations. Because Armstrong was considered the sole authority on doctrine, while he was alive church leaders could simply defer to him if a doctrinal question arose. I could simply say to the questioning minister or member, "God will reveal that to Mr. Armstrong if it is important. God works through Mr. Armstrong, and if it is God's will to change something, he will show Mr. Armstrong."

But with Armstrong's death, we could no longer defer to him. Personally, at the time of Armstrong's death, I did not believe there were any major errors in Armstrong's teachings. Minor things, yes, and we could deal with them—but certainly nothing substantial. Faithfulness to Scripture and to truth, however, would soon turn my world upside down.

The Holy Spirit worked relentlessly in our hearts through the Word of God to right our capsized church. As I reflect on my experiences in the Worldwide Church of God, I find that there are several principles that can help protect a church from doctrinal aberration and legalism. I offer the following "cult-proofing" strategies for any Christian church or ministry as a hedge from drifting into an exclusivist, body-dividing spirit.

STRATEGY 1: IN ANY CHRISTIAN LIFE AND COMMUNITY, THE WORD OF GOD MUST BE THE BASIS OF FAITH AND PRACTICE

God comes to us through his Word. All other ways in which God speaks to his people spring from, and are measured by, the touchstone of the testimony of Scripture. *Heresy cannot survive forever in a church that is committed to allowing the Bible to guide its faith and correct its tradition.* In the Worldwide Church of God, the death of Herbert Armstrong ended his tight rein on doctrine and scriptural interpretation, and the power of the Word of God was unleashed to breathe spiritual renewal and change lives.

Not a Jigsaw Puzzle

God does not ask his people to worry about things that are obscure. If we will only plant the things that are simple and clear in our hearts, they will bear fruit for eternal life. The obscure parts of the Bible will take care of themselves when we rest in the eternal embrace of the Lord.

The Bible is the testimony of the grace and glory of God in the face of Jesus Christ. We can gratefully affirm that God has designed the human heart to love a mystery. That is part of the creative nature he has shared with humanity. The unfolding mystery of God is something his glorified children have the indescribable blessing to enjoy for eternity. But our inherent love of mystery and discovery can be a trap when we use it to turn the Bible into a sort of jigsaw puzzle that only "insiders" can understand. Herbert Armstrong believed he was the one God had "raised up" to put all the pieces of the puzzle together. The plain truth of the grace of God manifest in Jesus Christ for our salvation is the greatest mystery of all. We can be thoroughly content with it.

Historic Witness of the Church

The Holy Spirit works in the context of the community of faith, not in the context of detached individuals. When people come to believe that the Spirit is leading them into a path contrary to the Spirit's witness in the history of the church, they are on the wrong path. The Holy Spirit guides the universal church primarily and fundamentally by means of the Scriptures, and the Spirit never contradicts the Spirit's own witness in the Bible. Herbert Armstrong's fundamental premise was that the truth had long lay "buried" until God raised him up, and that all other Christian churches were hopelessly deceived.

In this context, Christians do well to separate essentials from peripherals. By the fourth century, Christians had come to general consensus about the biblically rooted essentials upon which their faith had all along been based. These are reflected in the Nicene Creed, formulated in A.D. 381 at Constantinople:

THE NICENE CREED

We believe in one God, the Father, the Almighty, maker of heaven and earth, of all that is, seen and unseen.

We believe in one Lord, Jesus Christ, the only Son of God, eternally begotten of the Father, God from God, Light from Light, true God from true God, begotten, not made, of one Being with the Father. Through him all things were made. For us and for our salvation he came down from heaven: by the power of the Holy Spirit he became incarnate from the Virgin Mary, and was made man. For our sake he was crucified under Pontius Pilate; he suffered death and was buried. On the third day he rose again in accordance with the Scriptures; he ascended into heaven and is seated at the right hand of the Father. He will come again in glory to judge the living and the dead, and his kingdom will have no end.

We believe in the Holy Spirit, the Lord, the giver of life, who proceeds from the Father. With the Father and the Son he is worshiped and glorified. He has spoken through the Prophets.

We believe in one holy, all-embracing, and apostolic Church.

We look for the resurrection of the dead, and the life of the world to come. Amen.

The Definition of the Union of the Divine and Human Natures in the Person of Christ, formulated at the Council of Chalcedon in 451, expressed the Christian belief, derived from the biblical witness, that Jesus Christ is fully God and fully man, one person "in two natures, without confusion, without change, without division, without separation, the distinction of natures being in no way annulled by the union but rather the characteristics of each nature being preserved and coming together to form one person and subsistence."

The essentials of the Nicene Creed were also later articulated in what are called the Apostles' Creed and the Creed of Athanasius. Recognizing our unity in these basics of our Christian faith (along with their implied truths, reaffirmed by the Reformation, of 1) salvation by grace alone through faith and 2) the authority of Scripture), why must it be so difficult for us to receive one another in grace despite our differences in other, nonessential matters? What a glorious day it would be if we Christians could learn to live by the maxim we often recite: *In essentials, unity; in nonessentials, liberty; in all things charity.*

Planks and Specks

It is tempting to use the Bible to correct others rather than leaving them to God and letting the Bible correct *us.* Jesus tells us that we should get the planks out of our own eyes before we try to get the specks out of our brothers' eyes (Matt. 3:5). Jesus is telling us how to rightly look at things. We are asked to see our own sin as worse and needing more attention than our brother's sin. Do something about yourself first, Jesus says, then worry about your brother. And you may just find that when you can finally see clearly, that the speck has taken care of itself. A personal experience drove this lesson home to me.

There was a period in my life when I felt overwhelmed with family problems. For various reasons, I had begun to feel that my family was hopelessly out of control. "This is not how a Christian family should be," I prayed. "Help me to take charge and get this mess straightened out." The level of conflict seemed unbearable and intolerable, and I tried every method I knew to get things "under control."

One day it dawned on me (I have to think God put the thought in my head) that the real problem I was having here was not with my family but with me. I was trying to get everybody else to behave the way *I* felt they should, the way that made *me* comfortable and happy, instead of taking a good look at the way I was behaving.

What was I doing wrong? The first thing, ironically, was that I was preoccupied with what I was doing wrong. That is, I was preoccupied with my fear of failing. More precisely, I was afraid that others would perceive me as failing in leading my family as an ordained minister and denomination leader should.

In an interview with *Leadership*, Richard Foster said, "That's one of the great values of reading the saints. They had this utter vulnerability to fail by human standards."[1] That is such a freeing insight. The great men and women of God did not take themselves as seriously as I was taking myself. They saw themselves realistically in the light of the glory of God's grace. Thomas à Kempis wrote, "A humble understanding of yourself is a surer way to God than a profound searching after knowledge."[2]

That was my problem. My reputation, my pride, my sense of personal control over my world and my environment was more important to me than listening to the voice of God. God's will for my life, for what he wanted to do with me, was hidden by my desperate and futile struggle to get the people around me "under control." When I released them to God's care and gave myself and my sin to him, my family situation began to improve. The intolerable burden of trying to please people began to be lifted, and the peace of God's gracious touch began to reorder my entire perspective. In *Life Together*, Dietrich Bonhoeffer observes:

> Because Christ stands between me and others, I dare not desire direct fellowship with them. As only Christ can speak to me in such a way that I may be saved, so others, too, can be saved only by Christ himself. This means that I must release the other person from every attempt of mine to regulate, coerce, and dominate him with my love. The other person needs to retain his independence of me;

to be loved for what he is, as one for whom Christ became man, died, and rose again, for whom Christ bought forgiveness of sins and eternal life.[3]

Bonhoeffer was right. I had to learn that my relationship with those around me was not direct, but through Jesus. Only when I was rerooted in Jesus did the relationships in my family begin to heal and blossom. And it has been glorious to behold what the Lord does when I lose myself in him. Bonhoeffer continues:

> Because Christ has long since acted decisively for my brother, before I could begin to act, I must leave him his freedom to be Christ's; I must meet him only as the person that he already is in Christ's eyes.[4]

The Worldwide Church of God was unable to leave Christian churches their freedom to be Christ's. Much of the church's mass media evangelism was aimed at efforts to convince other Christians that they must cease their current Christian traditions and take up those of Herbert Armstrong:

> If you have sincerely repented and desire to live by every Word of God, you will begin to observe *God's* Holy Sabbath day—commonly called *Saturday*—the same commanded day Christ and His Apostles kept! You will **withdraw at once from all fellowship with this world's false churches** Satan has deceived into **observing Sunday,** a day which God *never* commanded.[5]

Rather than evangelize unbelievers, the Worldwide Church of God targeted the Christian world, which it considered to be unbelieving on the basis of the Sabbath doctrine. The Bible became a tool to correct not ourselves, but others. It was not until the death of Herbert Armstrong, and with him the myth that he was specially anointed by God to restore all truth, that our fellowship became fertile soil for the implanted Word to begin its transforming work.

STRATEGY 2: CENTER EVERY FACET OF PERSONAL AND BODY LIFE AROUND BELIEVING PRAYER

An authentic life of prayer keeps us in relationship with God and oriented toward seeking his will. Without believing prayer in the lives of its leaders and members, as well as prayers of intercession from the wider Christian community, I cannot imagine that the Worldwide Church of God would have been ready for God's healing touch.

Still, a caution is in order: Prayer must not be allowed to degenerate into a mere duty, or be restricted to stereotypical methods and paradigms. Henri Nouwen once described prayer in this way: "Prayer is first of all listening to God. It's openness. God is always speaking; he's always doing something. . . . Prayer in its most basic sense is just entering into an attitude of saying, 'Lord, what are you saying to me?' "[6]

The Worldwide Church of God consistently taught the value of meaningful, heartfelt prayer. But in order to have one's prayers answered, there were conditions: "The Bible reveals *seven basic conditions* which you should fulfill to be certain of *answered prayers.*"[7] The conditions expounded were biblically defensible enough:

- Know God's will.
- Believe God.
- Obey God.
- Fear and humility.
- Be fervent.
- Be persistent.
- Use Christ's name.

But like so many teachings of Armstrongism, there is the big *if*. Either you measure up to these seven points, or don't expect God to hear you. The lesson on prayer concludes: "If you faithfully conform to these seven *conditions of answered prayer*—with God's help, you may then have *absolute confidence* that God will hear and answer your prayers."[8]

What happens to folks who don't quite conform so well to the conditions? They should keep trying, church literature explained, believing God is merciful and patient. The idea sounds innocent enough, but it resulted in a lot of frustration. It was frustrating because it was founded on the premise that prayer is primarily about getting things from God. Therefore, if your prayer isn't answered—that is, you don't get what you asked for—then in which of the conditions have you failed? Is your obedience faltering? Are you not humble enough? Are you not fervent enough? Your focus shifts from intimacy with God to the quality of your own spiritual condition. You naturally feel God is not hearing you, that you must not be close to him, and that you have little hope of seeing that change.

For most of my life, I thought prayer was primarily about asking God to do things and then thanking God for the things he has done. I don't mean in a selfish way. I mean like asking God to heal people. To protect people. To make things work out all right. To help me quit sinning, and so on. You know the kind of prayers I'm talking about.

Intimacy with God

Until I began to study and experience prayer in a wonderful seminary class conducted by Richard Foster, it had never really occurred to me that prayer was about far more than making requests of God. The Bible teaches us that prayer is *being in the presence of God*. It involves not only asking for what we need but also listening to God and just being with God—just plain spending time with him, sometimes without saying anything, just like we do with our friends or family members. It involves an actual *relationship*, entering into God's presence not only to talk, but to simply *be there*, and to hear what God has to say to *me*.

In an interview with *Leadership*, Richard Foster said, "The problem with describing prayer as *speaking* to God is that it implies we are still in control. But in listening, we let go."[9] In looking back over the past eleven years since Herbert Armstrong's death, I now realize that God was teaching me to "let go," to relinquish control. As one doctrinal change led to another, I began to realize that my world, my life, my belief system, nearly everything I held dear and secure, were quite out of control. I didn't know where to go or what to do. I could only cling to the Scriptures and ask God to take control.

Slowly I began to understand that I could not rely on anything I thought I had known about the Bible, about doctrine, about church history, and especially about the Worldwide Church of God in which I had grown up. The frightening realization that nothing I had believed in was secure except God himself slowly gave way to God's gracious assurance that he is quite sufficient. He is my all in all.

Prayer as a Dialogue

When I learned that real prayer is a dialogue, not a monologue, my life began to change. Not because I was "trying harder" or struggling "more mightily" against sin, but simply because I was beginning to walk with God. "Lord, put in my heart what you want to pray through me" is a prayer I have learned to practice. "Lord, teach me what you would have me learn from your Word today" is another.

As long as I thought of prayer as a Christian duty or as a series of requests instead of a joyfully anticipated communion with my Lord, Teacher, and Savior, it was never fully satisfying. Dutiful prayer was a chore, something I *had* to do in order to *be right with God*. The focus tended to be on myself, on my need to do right things that pleased God in order that I might measure up to his standards so that he would respond to my requests. That approach smothers the joy of prayer, the free and abandoned intimacy with the Lord of my life. It shatters the peace of sharing everything with him, of laying my heart and soul bare before him, inviting him to come in and reorder my passions and habits, knowing he knows every dark and foul corner of my corrupt heart and loves me anyway, and waiting in silence for him to merge my will to his.

For prayer to become another rule, something to "get in" in order to alleviate feelings of guilt, another measure of whether you are doing everything you ought to be doing if you "expect God to help your life go right" is to diminish the vitality and joy of a prayer-filled life.

Nevertheless, the fact that regular prayer was upheld as a vital ingredient of the Christian life set the stage for WCG members to take their pain and frustration about massive changes in church doctrine to the right place—to the throne of God. In his presence, they were able to be molded and shaped—taught to be patient, to give emotions time to catch up with intellect, and to trust him to bring them and their church through its time of trial.

STRATEGY 3: NEVER BE AFRAID TO FACE THE TRUTH

As God worked in my heart during my years in Herbert Armstrong's administration, I began to sense that reality was in conflict with my assumptions about my church and its leader. While Herbert Armstrong was alive, however, I would not allow myself to even question or doubt his authority or role as "God's only anointed end-time apostle." As in any authoritarian-style organization, loyalty quickly rises to the top of the value system. Nothing was more important than loyalty to Armstrong and to the church. Herbert Armstrong was God's man, so loyalty to Armstrong was loyalty to God.

When Armstrong died, his "aura" of power and authority slowly began to dissipate for me as an impediment to bare honesty. For some time, it was as though he still had a grip on my leg from his grave. Eventually (for me, it took about three years and several struggles with Armstrong's doctrinal errors, including his Trinitarian heresy), his grip weakened, and the fog of misplaced loyalty began to clear. Only then, it seems, was I emotionally free to begin to respond to the prompting of the Holy Spirit to face issues about my church and its history with pure honesty, without making excuses or concocting rationalizations.

I believe a spiritually healthy church or group is honest with itself. Where there is pretense, there is spiritual sickness. Jesus is the Truth, and when his disciples are committed to him, they are committed to truth. Only when we face the truth can there be freedom in Christ. Only when we face the truth can there be healing and forgiveness. Only when we face the truth can we stand before God ready for his regenerating and transforming work in our deepest parts. I suggest the following "litmus test" for honesty in any Christian organization:

- *Face the truth about yourself.* You are a sinner. God knows it and you know it. Be brutally honest with yourself and with God about that.
- *Face the truth about your group.* No group, including yours, is the one and only "faithful remnant." Your group is not the most important group on earth. Its mission is not the most important mission on earth. There will not be a "greater reward" for members of your group. Your group is not "more special" than other parts of the body of Christ. God loves you and every member in your group, but he can, in fact, get by without your group.
- *Face the truth about your leader.* No leader is infallible. No leader has "all the truth." No leader has been raised up by God to bring "new" truth that has "never before been understood." No leader has a special dispensation from God to sin. No leader is the only true servant of God.
- *Face the truth about your questions.* If you have questions, admit them to yourself. Don't be afraid to explore the possible answers. You don't have to reach final conclusions; you just have to live in the real world. To suppress your questions or hide from them only sets you up for even greater disillusionment and grief later.

- *Don't be afraid to seek the truth.* Truth may hurt, but it is the best medicine for healthy living. Many former WCG members chose to cover their ears rather than hear the truth about Herbert Armstrong's errors. Many refused to read any church literature explaining doctrinal changes and the need for them. Whatever the emotional reason for refusing to examine facts, honesty was sacrificed for comfort. Truth stands up to examination. There is no need to fear it. If your belief is false, it is far better to face it and change it than to cling to it. "You shall know the truth, and the truth shall make you free," Jesus said. The temporary pain of facing the truth is well worth the joy of freedom that it brings.

John Dawson, founder of the International Racial Reconciliation Coalition, has said that only we Christians have the freedom to be honest about our true situations. It is only when things are uncovered that the blood of Christ can be applied.

Taking Ourselves Too Seriously

We all tend to see ourselves as the center of the universe. Even after we give ourselves to God, we are still inclined to view things through the lens of our own feelings, desires, passions, habits, and viewpoints. And that's just the problem. The Christian walk is one of taking up our cross (symbolic of dying to self and living for Christ) and following Jesus (into his life of self-sacrifice, humility, and love). When we take our own opinions too seriously, we take ourselves too seriously. And when we take ourselves too seriously, we stop taking God seriously enough.

"I could be wrong" is a truism that should be part of every person's belief system and vocabulary. We believe others should live by it, but we tend to reject it as a guide for ourselves. Thomas Kelly wisely observed, "For humility and holiness are twins in the astonishing birth of obedience in the human heart."[10]

If we could sense the reality of the presence of God when we allow our dogmatism to balloon, perhaps we would learn to insert the popping pin ourselves.

Legalism Breeds Hypocrisy

If I am a biblical legalist, I am a hypocrite. The two are fundamentally synonymous. That is because legalists eventually have to extend to themselves the liberty to break their own code. This is what they never want to admit, either to themselves or to others. One of the first steps we must take to break out of the prison of legalism is to admit that we have, in reality, two sets of rules: one for others and one for ourselves. (Pity the poor rare legalist who actually lives by his own rules—his disease may be even worse.)

Herbert Armstrong was not always known for living by the principles he taught. He taught simplicity, but he was known for luxurious living. He taught rigid adherence to the Sabbath, holy days, and meat laws, but those close to him knew that he made himself an exception when the situation warranted it. He taught that it was sinful to take pharmaceuticals, but he did so himself. I do not say this to vilify Herbert Armstrong but to illustrate that human beings are rarely capable of successfully living up to their own codes of conduct. For this reason legalism could rightly be called the mother of hypocrisy.

God knows those who are his. We Christians seem to have a compulsive need to make boundaries that Jesus does not make. And sometimes our boundary making leaves us outside of the place where Jesus is working. Thank God, the Holy Spirit does not consult denominational polity and doctrinal nuance before he meets men, women, and children where they are and draws them into the everlasting kingdom.

STRATEGY 4: BE COMMITTED TO JESUS, NOT TO IDEALS

"I stand on my principles," we like to say. It makes us feel good about ourselves, like courageous heroes. But principles are not people, and Jesus commands us to love our neighbors, not our principles.

When we commit ourselves to ideals, we are committing ourselves to someone's, perhaps our own, set of standards or paradigms that guide and shape our decisions. Jesus, on the other hand, says, "Come to me, and I will give you rest." He says, "Take up your cross and follow me." We have to remember that he is a person, not a rule book. And he is God. Our opinion is not equal to his opinion. Our sizing up of a situation isn't on the same level as his sizing up of a situation. His opinion is Truth. He sizes up all situations perfectly.

Our commitment, therefore, must be to Jesus, the man who is God, not to our assessment of what we assume to be the true state of affairs. Jesus will guide his people, but he does expect them to come to him, and he does expect them to take him seriously.

When we face a crisis of faith and identity, we become confused, frightened, and depressed. We find ourselves unsure about who we are or what we believe. The harder we try to "figure it all out," the worse it seems to become. The answer is simple, almost too simple. But it is the right answer, indeed the only answer: Leave the conflict to Jesus. Rest in his love. Philip Yancey puts it well:

> Jesus came to earth "full of grace and truth," says the gospel of John, and that phrase makes a good summary of his message. First, grace: in contrast to those who tried to complicate the faith and petrify it with legalism, Jesus preached a simple message of God's love. For no reason—certainly not because we deserve it—God has decided to extend to us love that comes free of charge, no strings attached, "on the house."[11]

God does not wait until we deserve it, until we are in just the right spiritual state of mind. He loves us, pure and simple. He is looking for any excuse to help us. The reason we are experiencing the crisis of faith and identity is because Jesus is at work in us. He is challenging our assumptions so that he can show us the truth about who we are and what can be trusted. I love the beautiful words of Jean-Pierre de Caussade:

> So God hides himself in order to raise souls up to that perfect faith which will discover him under every kind of disguise. For once they know God's secret, disguise is useless. They say: "See him! There he is, behind the wall, looking through the trellis, in at the window!"[12]

The way to survive the storm is to fly to the safe harbor of his loving embrace. Remember the truth you know: Jesus died for you while you were still a sinner. He loves you. He accepts you. He will lead you. Give the conflict to him, and take your rest, trusting him to see you through. Don't expect an immediate answer. The psalmist knew the value of waiting for the Lord (cf. Ps. 130:5). It is during the wait that your Savior is reordering your assumptions and regenerating your heart so that you may finally rest completely in his perfect care. De Caussade paints a wonderfully mundane illustration:

> When one is led by a guide who takes one through unknown country by night, across ground without any clearly defined paths, going wherever he fancies without asking advice or disclosing his intentions, what is there but to surrender to him?[13]

STRATEGY 5: REMEMBER THAT THE GOSPEL DOES NOT NEED "IMPROVING," "UPDATING," OR "RESTORING"

The gospel is the power of God for the salvation of all who believe, Paul declared in Romans 1:13. There was nothing vague or incomplete about it. Paul wrote to the Corinthians that he had passed on to them the gospel just as it had been given to him:

> Now I would remind you, brothers and sisters, of the good news that I proclaimed to you, which you in turn received, in which also you stand, through which also you are being saved, if you hold firmly to the message that I proclaimed to you—unless you have come to believe in vain.
>
> For I handed on to you as of first importance what I in turn had received: that Christ died for our sins in accordance with the scriptures, and that he was buried, and that he was raised on the third day in accordance with the scriptures, and that he appeared to Cephas, then to the twelve. (1 Cor. 15:1–5, NRSV)

The gospel has not been lost for nineteen centuries, as Herbert Armstrong declared.[14] And it was not, as Armstrong declared, "suppressed and replaced by man's gospel about Christ."[15] Armstrong taught that the true gospel was the message "Christ himself preached," that is, the gospel of the kingdom of God, and that by the middle of the second century "there appeared an entirely different type of church calling itself Christian, but in the main preaching its own gospel ABOUT Christ, not the gospel of Christ."[16]

For Armstrong, this contrived gospel conspiracy provided another major plank in his condemnation of all other Christian churches: "Because they *rejected* Christ's gospel 1,900 years ago, the world had to supplant something else in its place. They had to invent a *counterfeit!*"[17] Armstrong's manufactured dilemma (the gospel Christ preached vs. a gospel about Christ), is set straight in Philip Yancey's simple words:

> Jesus' statements about himself (I and the Father are one; I have the power to forgive sins; I will rebuild the temple in three days) were unprecedented and got him into constant trouble. Indeed, his teaching was so intertwined with his person that many of his words could not have outlived him; the grand claims died with him on the cross. Disciples

who had followed him as a master returned to their former lives, muttering sadly, "We had hoped that he was the one who was going to redeem Israel." It took the Resurrection to turn the proclaimer of truth into the one proclaimed.[18]

In the New Testament the apostles are unanimous in the essential content of the gospel proclamation—Jesus is the One whom God sent to redeem humanity (cf. Acts 2:36; 10:42–43; 13:33; 1 John 5:10–12). This is the grand truth that Herbert Armstrong missed in his attempt to interpret the Bible literally according to his own perspective without testing his views against the witness of the Spirit in the history of the church.

Armstrong missed the fundamental biblical truth that the person of Jesus and the kingdom of God cannot be disconnected. Humans come into the kingdom only *in Jesus*, and not of their own accord, on their own power, or on their own standing before God, but only on the basis of *Jesus'* standing before God. Jesus proclaims the kingdom; Jesus proclaims himself. Apart from Jesus, there is no entrance for us into the kingdom. For us, the kingdom and Jesus are thoroughly inseparable. The kingdom exists before the incarnation, during the incarnation, and after the incarnation; and precisely because of the incarnation, we are invited to *enter the kingdom* through the door God has provided—Jesus Christ.[19]

Armstrong's belief that God had called him personally to restore the true gospel reflected his misunderstanding of the fundamental nature of Jesus Christ. On this house of cards, Armstrong built his thesis that he was God's specially called messenger to preach the true gospel. Imagine what would have happened if Armstrong had submitted himself to an accountability group or had belonged to a pastoral association and had discussed his ideas with his peers, trusting Jesus to teach him through the normal scriptural avenues of Christian discipleship. His error would most likely have been exposed, and perhaps he could have stayed on a course of unity with the body of Christ.

STRATEGY 6: DON'T COMPROMISE WITH THE TRUTH, BUT LET GRACE AND LOVE SEASON YOUR MANNER

As I went through the crisis of massive doctrinal change in my church, the Holy Spirit was granting me a fresh sense of conviction about the truly important things of life. The Scriptures began to speak to my heart in a new and motivating way. I began to experience fresh and exciting love for God. As all this happened, I also began to experience a corresponding disgust for my past experience, which now seemed hollow and empty at best, perhaps even vile and sickening. I frequently felt angry when I thought about the deception that had held me captive, and I got even angrier when I thought about how I had helped add strands to the web of ignorance and confusion for others.

I sometimes found myself tempted to vent my anger with people who had not come as far down that path as God had brought me. To have done so would have succeeded only in driving them farther away from the light into which God was bringing me and deeper into the darkness I was attacking. God desires that we be ministers of his grace, not ministers of our own pain and anger, to those still under the spell. Their assumptions must be challenged, yes, but Jesus in us comes to others in love, not in anger, impatience, or pride.

I am reminded of the woman at the well. Jesus' approach to her was to speak the truth in love. That approach always works best, because it is God's approach. God isn't selfish. He doesn't need an emotional venting. He speaks the truth in love. And when we let him have his way with us, we can speak the truth in love too.

What we say to others must be true. We must not compromise with that. But it must also be spoken in love and in great patience or it will do more harm than good. "A word aptly spoken is like apples of gold in settings of silver" (Prov. 25:11). Henri Nouwen wrote of his feelings when a former student came to visit during his seven-month stay at a Trappist monastery in upstate New York: "I discover in myself the desire to make him feel, see, and experience all I have done in the last four months, but realize that God touches each one in a different way."[20]

Richard Foster cites four ways we tend to rush ahead when attempting to bring truth to others:

1. Ignoring the rituals of acquaintanceship.
2. Trying to get people interested in our message before they know we are interested in their lives.
3. Trying to bring them to a decision before they are ready for a decision.
4. Trying to bring people into a teaching before they can receive the teaching.[21]

Jesus told his disciples, "I still have many things to say to you, but you cannot bear them now" (John 16:12, NRSV). God knows the right timing. When we learn to release people to him, we can begin to grow in sensitivity to his timing. Henri Nouwen wrote: "I realize that compassion is not mine but God's gift to me. I cannot embrace the world, but God can."[22]

STRATEGY 7: REMEMBER THAT A JUDGMENTAL HEART IS WORSE THAN POOR THEOLOGY

After all the Worldwide Church of God has been through and the price we have paid for right theology, what I'm going to say here may seem strange. But it has to be said: There are worse things than poor theology.

Some Christians consider C. S. Lewis's allegorical salvation of the Calormene soldier in *The Last Battle* a theological error on Lewis's part.[23] I don't. When I consider the narrow-minded, exclusivist, and self-centered spirit that characterized my church and compare it on one hand to the careful, fastidious religion of the covenant-faithful people who rejected and opposed Jesus, and on the other hand to the Teacher's words about whom he came to save (cf. John 6:40), I can only conclude that the Lord knows those who are his a lot better than we humans do.

I cannot imagine that the Gadarene demoniac had his creedal theology down pat before he began to proclaim the name of Jesus to all the surrounding region. Christian history shows us that it is very easy for us to allow our pursuit of "orthodox" theology to derail our commitment to takes up our cross and follow Jesus, especially his command that we love one another. Jesus readily accepted men, women, and children to whom we would not even have spoken. He also accepted the saints of the Old Testament, who never heard the name of Jesus yet trusted themselves to Yahweh (who was none other than the great I-AM, the Blessed Trinity) for mercy and blessing.

Philip Yancey once wrote of Henri Nouwen's remarkable commitment to the care of a young profoundly retarded man named Adam. As I read Yancey's article, I was at once touched by the sheer power of Nouwen's unselfish humility and stunned by Yancey's sublime observation:

> It had been difficult for him at first, he said. Physical touch, affection, and the messiness of caring for an uncoordinated person did not come easily. But he had learned to love Adam, truly to love him. In the process he had learned what it must be like for God to love us—spiritually uncoordinated, retarded, able to respond with what must seem to God like inarticulate grunts and groans.[24]

I praise God for that graphic and undeniable image! Isn't it descriptive of our true spiritual condition? Yet, as though blind to the depth of our own need and backwardness, we happily draw our lines and exclude one another, as though Jesus made us judge and jury of the hearts of his loved ones. (And the beauty and power of God's grace is that he will forgive even our divisive arrogance and pride when we acknowledge our sin and place ourselves at his disposal.)

I believe C. S. Lewis was right about the Calormene soldier. That soldier's heart was the heart of a Narnian, and he loved and served Aslan even though he didn't know of Aslan the way Narnians knew of Aslan. The point is that Aslan knew *him*. The Lord knows those who are his. I believe that if my Lord saves *even me*—a pitiful, struggling, spiritually deformed, retarded, and stubborn child (and he does)—that he can save anybody. And he does. *"He is the atoning sacrifice for our sins, and not only for ours but also for the sins of the whole world"* (1 John 2:2).

> The Lord is not slow in keeping his promise, as some understand slowness. He is patient with you, not wanting anyone to perish, but everyone to come to repentance. (2 Peter 3:9)

It is indeed an exquisite spiritual intoxication to belong to the "right" church, hold the "right" doctrines, and say the "right" things, and enjoy the warm feeling of a smug superiority toward fellow believers. We can become so drunk on our own "rightness" and "holy difference" that we stumble about in our spinning spiritual world blissfully unaware of our true spiritual condition.

I believe this spirit of condemnation lay at the heart of the sin of the Worldwide Church of God. While we professed to have the "truth" and be the only faithful church, we condemned and dismissed the faith of anyone whose doctrinal package did not match ours. That is hypocrisy; those who love Jesus love those Jesus loves. At the root of hypocrisy lies idolatry: worshiping the creature (in this case, *ourselves* and our doctrines) more than the Creator.

The true fruit of Christian lives was irrelevant to us. "Oh sure," we liked to say, "those professing Christian people may do a lot of good things. But what good are all their so-called good works? They refuse to keep the test commandment—the Sabbath." To the Worldwide Church of God, the seventh-day Sabbath (along with the annual old covenant holy days) was the identifying sign of true Christians. But to Jesus, love for one another was the identifying sign.

In the Worldwide Church of God, we claimed to be the only faithful followers of Jesus, yet we disobeyed the very command he gave that identifies his true followers: "By this everyone will know that you are my disciples, if you have love one for another" (John 13:35, NRSV). I don't believe that the love Jesus commands here can be equated with an ecclesiastical pronouncement that somebody else's profession of faith in the saving blood of Jesus Christ is worthless due to doctrinal differences. I pray I will never again belong to a church that dares take the prerogative of God to declare that another Christian's faith is false on the basis of a disagreement over rules of conduct or details of history.

Jesus called sinners to repentance. He saves the poor, the uneducated, the illiterate, the infirm. He doesn't save only the articulate and bright and those who get good marks on their theology tests. He calls men, women, and children into the community of faith he calls his own body. He does not call them into some carefully crafted organization designed to keep out and persecute the undesirables who dare view a certain exalted bit of theological esoterica with less reverence than they "ought."

The sin of the Worldwide Church of God lay not only with its doctrinal error, but even more seriously with its arrogant, self-righteous, in-your-face declaration that it had the corner on the doctrinal market. Its sin was in its high-and-mighty condemnation of the people of God who did not interpret Scripture in the same way the Worldwide Church of God did. Its sin was in its disobedience to Jesus' command, "Love one another."

Lest anyone misunderstand, I do not mean to say that doctrine is unimportant. I believe right doctrine is crucial to the spiritual health of the body of Christ. But I also believe that the blood of Jesus Christ is powerful enough even to wash his children clean from doctrinal error.

The thief on the cross did not have to be schooled and tested on his grasp of Trinitarian theology before Jesus declared, "You will be with me in paradise." He saw the Lord, and he believed. That was that.

"That You Love One Another"

A good way for a church to insulate itself from adopting a self-centered agenda is to commit to partnership with a Christian organization of a different tradition. To do so constitutes an act of giving liberty to Christians of other traditions and of looking past distinctives in order to build the kingdom. It forces us to place Jesus' command and the kingdom of God ahead of personal comfort zones, personal power, and personal agenda.

Partnership demands trust—trust in God to save people whose tradition is not the same as our own, trust in God to do mighty kingdom work through people who have doctrinal beliefs with which we do not agree, and trust in God to teach us truth about his will through people who hold certain beliefs that irritate us.

To work together across denominational lines as Christian brothers and sisters does not mean we have to hold identical beliefs on all points. But it does mean that we have taken seriously Jesus' command to his followers that we love one another.

Thomas à Kempis, a man not unconcerned about right theology, put theological learning in the right perspective:

> Jesus: . . . But woe to those who spend their lives in rooting out esoteric learning, caring little about how to serve me. The time will come when Christ, the Teacher of teachers, the Lord of angels, will appear to conduct the final exam; that is, to examine each person's conscience. . . . To some I speak what is plain to all; to others, what is for them alone. To some I make myself known sweetly in symbol and metaphor; to others, I reveal my mysteries in striking clarity. A book teaches one lesson, but it does not teach everyone equally, for deep within you, I am the Teacher of truth, the Searcher of the heart, the Reader of thought, the Mover of deeds, giving understanding to each person as I see fit.[25]

God is in the business of loving, forgiving, and perfecting. The bumper sticker says, "Jesus saves." It's true. That is what Jesus does. And Jesus' saving power doesn't depend on neat doctrine. It depends on Jesus. I have to believe the Lord can and will, in his good time, straighten out the doctrinal problems of everybody who loves him. (And only a fool or a liar claims he and his tradition have no doctrinal problems.) But a heart that doesn't love and forgive is a heart in which Jesus doesn't live, and such hearts, by their own choice and preference, won't enter the kingdom of God.

CONCLUSION

The Holy Spirit has performed a miraculous and historic work in the church founded by Herbert W. Armstrong. The essential vessels of the Spirit's work in the Worldwide Church of God were the Word of God, the gracious gift of a commitment to truth and holy living, and a perpetual covering of prayer from Christians outside as well as inside the small denomination. The journey of the Worldwide Church of God may hold certain lessons and suggest certain strategies for the body of Christ at large. This book is my attempt to propose a few possibilities. I conclude with the words of William Temple:

> Our dignity is that we are children of God, capable of communion with God, the object of the love of God— displayed to us on the Cross—and destined for eternal fellowship with God. Our true value is not what we are worth in ourselves, but what we are worth to God, and that worth is bestowed upon us by the utterly gratuitous love of God.[26]

Praise God for his mercy, his faithfulness, his power, and his infinite love, of which the Worldwide Church of God is but one undeserving vessel.

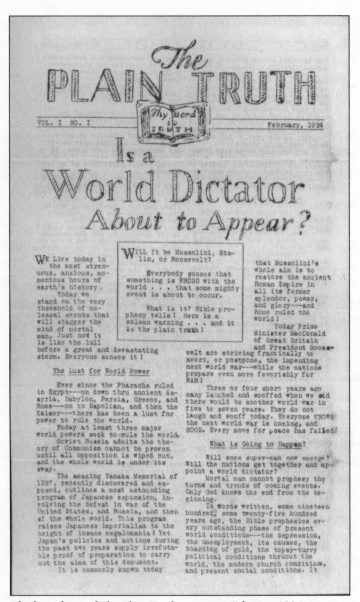

The first edition of The Plain Truth *magazine, February 1934.*

March 1958

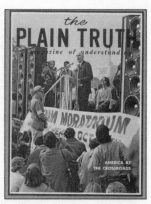

November 1969

August 1980

April 1990

July 1999

The changing face of The Plain Truth *through five decades.*

Joseph W. Tkach Sr. (left) and J. Michael Feazell.

Feazell (left) and Joseph Tkach Jr.

APPENDICES

1.

CHANGED PARADIGMS IN THE WORLDWIDE CHURCH OF GOD

Old Paradigm	New Paradigm
Mass media evangelism	Relational evangelism
Prophecy ministry: Warning to repent in order to escape Great Tribulation	Gospel ministry: Invitation to believe the gospel and enter the kingdom
Unity achieved through control	Unity experienced through common faith in Jesus Christ
Primary goal: Endure to the end	Primary goal: Love the Lord
Condemnation of all non-WCG Christian churches as "false churches," "churches of this world," or "churches of the devil"	Recognition of the church universal and embracing all believers in Jesus Christ as spiritual brothers and sisters
Pastors as religious policemen	Pastors as equippers of the saints
Focus of proclamation: Obey the law	Focus of proclamation: Believe and live the gospel
Pursuit of personal piety, holiness, and discipline rooted in law keeping	Pursuit of personal piety, holiness, and discipline rooted in authentic faith

Aversion to group prayer	Embracing of group prayer
Members forbidden to assemble for worship without an ordained elder present	Proliferation of small-group Bible study, prayer, and worship regardless of whether an ordained elder is present
Expressive worship strongly discouraged	Expressive worship permitted
Ecstatic experience not permitted	Ecstatic experience not forbidden, except in congregational worship service
"Faith once delivered to the saints" defined essentially in terms of Sabbatarianism	"Faith once delivered to the saints" defined essentially in terms of belief in the pure gospel

2.

Highlights of Worldwide Church of God Doctrinal Changes

Former Teaching	New Teaching	Date
Since God is our Healer, it is a sin to take pharmaceuticals and have surgery.	God does not forbid the use of pharmaceuticals or surgery.	3/87
The use of cosmetics is vanity and therefore sinful.	God does not forbid the use of cosmetics.	11/88
Birthday celebrations exalt the self and are therefore sinful.	God does not forbid birthday celebrations.	7/89
Interracial marriage is contrary to God's will.	God does not forbid interracial marriage.	7/90
The term "born again" refers to receiving the glorified body at the resurrection.	The term "born again" refers to conversion.	1/91
The kingdom of God will not appear until Christ's return.	The kingdom of God is present as well as future.	5/91

The gospel is the good news of the future kingdom of God to be established when Christ returns; it is not a message about the person of Christ.	The focus of the gospel is the good news about Jesus Christ.	5/91
The reward of the saved is to be literally born as a God into the God Family, to be Gods just as God is God, yet under his supreme authority.	The reward of the saved is to become children of God now and to receive glorified bodies like that of Jesus at the resurrection; it is not to become Gods in a family of Gods.	7/91
The cross is a pagan symbol: Jesus was crucified on a stake, not on a cross.	Jesus was most likely crucified on a cross; God does not forbid the use of the cross symbol for Christians.	5/93
Voting in civil elections is a denial of faith in God's sovereign reign and is therefore sinful.	God does not forbid voting in civil elections.	5/93
Using drawings depicting Jesus is sinful.	God does not forbid the use of drawings of Jesus.	5/93
The Trinity is a pagan invention the devil foisted off on the deceived and reprobate Roman Catholic Church.	The doctrine of the Trinity is true.	7/93
The new covenant will not be in force until the return of Christ.	The church is under the new covenant.	3/94
The Worldwide Church of God is the one and only true church of God, the faithful remnant.	All believers are true Christians.	4/94

Christians are required to tithe according to the law given to Israel: one tenth of gross income goes to the church, another tenth is kept by the Christian for required festival expenses, and another tenth (every third year in a cycle of seven) goes to the church to support the widows and needy.	The new covenant does not require the practice of tithing; rather, the Holy Spirit inspires a generous heart.	12/94
The seventh-day Sabbath, along with the seven annual holy days, is binding on Christians and is the sign between God and his only true and faithful church.	The new covenant does not require observance of the weekly Sabbath.	12/94
The dietary laws of Leviticus are binding on Christians.	The new covenant does not require observance of the clean and unclean meat laws.	1/95
The seventh-day Sabbath, along with the seven annual holy days, is binding on Christians and is the sign between God and his only true and faithful church.	The new covenant does not require observance of the seven annual holy days. The Lord's Supper is not restricted to once a year.	2/95
The United States and Britain are the modern descendants of the Israelite tribes of Ephraim and Manasseh, and knowledge of their identities is the master key to unlocking all of Bible prophecy.	The "lost ten tribes" doctrine cannot be proven and will no longer be taught. It is not the "master key" to unlocking Bible prophecy, but rather it obscures the true gospel.	7/95

3.

STATISTICAL SUMMARY

COMPARISON OF WORLDWIDE CHURCH OF GOD U.S.
STATISTICS FROM 1989 TO 2000

Chart 1

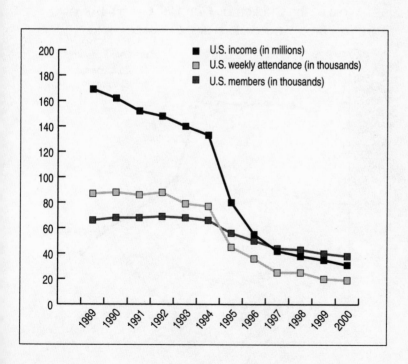

NOTES ON CHART 1

1. Worldwide Church of God U.S. income increased steadily until reaching its peak in 1989.
2. In the years 1989–2000, *income* declined from $168 million to $31.2 million, *weekly attendance* declined from 87,000 to 18,200, *membership* declined from 66,000 to 37,500.
3. Compare this chart with dates of doctrinal changes in appendix 2. The greatest declines occurred in 1995, immediately following the Sabbath and annual holy day change.
4. Immediately following the Sabbath and holy day change in 1995, total attendance fell below total number of members for the first time in the church's history. That situation has not changed.

Chart 2

WORLDWIDE CHURCH OF GOD U.S. CAREER PASTORS, BIVOCATIONAL PASTORS, CONGREGATIONS

■ Career pastors
□ Congregations
■ Bi-vocational pastors

5. Due to the sharp decline in income, by 1997 the church had ended its *World Tomorrow* television program, closed both campuses of Ambassador College, virtually ended its publishing ministry, and spun off *The Plain Truth* magazine into Plain Truth Ministries, an independent parachurch organization.

NOTES ON CHART 2

1. In the years 1989–2000, the number of *career pastors* declined from 458 to 120, the number of *bivocational* pastors increased from 0 to 177, and the number of *congregations* decreased slightly from 456 to 446.
2. Compare this chart with dates of doctrinal changes in appendix 2. The greatest decline in the number of career pastors occurred in 1995, immediately following the Sabbath and annual holy day change.
3. As the number of career pastors declined (due to a decline in financial support), the number of bivocational pastors increased.

WCG WORLD MEMBERSHIP FIGURES 2001

Africa: 135 congregations in 20 nations, 8,000 members, 11,000 in attendance

Australia, South Asia, and Oceania: 65 congregations in 23 nations, 3,500 members, 2,500 in attendance

Canada: 75 congregations, 6,000 members, 3,500 in attendance

Caribbean and Latin America: 60 congregations in 31 nations, 3,000 members, 2,000 in attendance

Europe and Middle East: 100 congregations in 31 nations, 5,500 members, 5,000 in attendance

Philippines and Northern Asia: 80 congregations in 4 nations, 4,000 members, 2,500 in attendance

United States: 475 congregations, 37,500 members, 18,500 in attendance

Worldwide totals: 990 congregations in 111 nations, 67,000 members, 51,000 in attendance

4.

PASTORAL LETTER FROM RICHARD J. FOSTER

*Regarding the Setting of Dates
for the Return of Christ*

HEART TO HEART: A Pastoral Letter from Richard J. Foster
November 1995

Dear Friends,

I write to you today out of pastoral concern. As the year 2000 draws near, we are seeing more and more end-time scenarios as apocalyptic zeal rises to fever pitch. There were early-bird predictions: Edgar C. Whisenant's *88 Reasons Why the Rapture Will Be In 1988* and a follow-up book *The Final Shout: Rapture Report 1989, 1990, 1991, 1992, 1993* . . . sold several million copies; South Korean Lee Jang Rim convinced followers around the globe that Christ would return in October 1992; and on the air and in his book, *1994*, the popular American radio Bible teacher Harold Camping targeted September 6 as the date for the final trump.

But the year 2000** is right now favored by most prophecy preachers—though it isn't clear whose calendar we are supposed to follow or why God favors round numbers! (Two heavy hitters on the apocalyptic scene have recently weighed in with their contributions to the subject: Hal Lindsey with *Planet Earth—2000 A.D.* and Pat Robertson with *The End of the Age*, a novel which is conveniently set in the year 2000.)

All of this is big business today in Christian bookstores and at the Christian Booksellers Convention. And in the general public, a recent prime-time series on ancient prophecies warned that futurists from Nostradamus to Edgar Cayce have targeted the year 2000 for the end of the world.

We are today awash in a sea of apocalyptic tabloid books. Not since the Millerite movement a century and a half ago has there been such a feeding frenzy over the end of the world. We can only expect it to increase.

We could let all this pass without comment except for two important factors:

One, apocalyptic speculation demeans the everlasting gospel of Jesus Christ. The church is constantly doing damage control as the predictions of these self-appointed prophets fall into public ridicule.

Two, it is confusing to many sincere people who want to be faithful disciples of Christ. Good people become sidetracked from the substantive issue of continuing to grow in grace into foolish conjectures about when the Rapture will occur, where the Antichrist will be born, and the like.

GAINING PERSPECTIVE

End-time speculations are nothing new. A little historical perspective may be helpful. Consider the following sampling:

**With these comments I am not referring to legitimate organizations that use the year 2000 as a target goal for their endeavors. The "AD 2000 and Beyond Movement" is one such group that uses this date to stimulate their evangelistic efforts. I applaud their work and that of other similar groups.

- In the second and third centuries Chiliasm (a name based on the Greek word in Rev. 20:3 which denotes the number 1000) predicted an early return of Christ and a millennial reign in Jerusalem. One leader in Pontius declared that the last judgment would come in two years, and his followers ceased to cultivate their fields and got rid of houses and goods. Another leader in Syria led his flock out into the wilderness to meet Christ.

- Second-century Montanists prophesied that there would be an early end to the world, that the New Jerusalem would "come down out of heaven from God," and that Jesus' Second Coming would occur at Pepuza, a village in the Phrygian region of Asia Minor.

- Doomsday hysteria erupted around the year 1000 as wandering hermit messiahs fanned into flame the hopes of marginalized peoples. When Jesus did not return, the people's expectations were dashed, and they were left in even greater misery and despair.

- Gerard of Poehlde was convinced that the 1000-year reign of Christ had begun with the ascent of Constantine to power, and so in 1147 he predicted that Satan would be released soon from bondage and would conquer the Church.

- The radical reformer Hans Hut predicted the return of Christ at Pentecost, 1528, and set about gathering 144,000 elect saints to prepare for this event. Another self-styled prophet, Melchior Hoffmann, set 1534 as the date and Strasbourg as the place for Christ's return. Both of these men died in prison with their prophecies unfulfilled and their disciples disillusioned.

- Apocalyptic passion fueled the Crusades, leaving a legacy of hate and suspicion that has lasted well into the twentieth century.

- In 1661 the "Fifth Monarchy Men" tried to hasten Jesus' Second Coming by attacking the restored Stuart monarchy.

This, they felt, would prove to God that "there was faith on the earth" and so Christ would return and establish his millennial reign in London. The sorry affair failed, and with the perpetrators jailed or beheaded, the movement fizzled.

- Postmillennial schemes were advanced by eighteenth-century American colonial leaders like Jonathan Edwards and Timothy Dwight. In the nineteenth century, Charles Finney was convinced that if people were "united all over the world, the millennium might be brought about in three months."

- William Miller, a pioneer of the Adventist movement, following painstaking study of Bible prophecies, declared that Christ would return in 1843. When that date passed without the expected Second Advent, he recalculated his data and set the date in 1844. Followers sold goods and properties and sat on a hill, waiting for an event that never occurred. You can imagine the resulting disillusionment.

COUNSELS FOR TODAY

In light of history and the contemporary apocalyptic fervor, I offer these counsels:

1. **Hold high "the blessed hope" of Jesus' return.** It is too precious a doctrine to be co-opted by self-proclaimed prophets who lack training in historical theology and biblical interpretation. Christ's *parousia* has always been and will always be the expectant hope of the people of God. Jesus' words are clear, "I will come again and will take you to myself, so that where I am, there you may be also" (John 14:3 [NRSV]).

2. **Reject the fallacy of date setting and place setting.** Friends, there simply is no "countdown to Armageddon." The future is contingent upon the give-and-take of God's initiative and our response. Faith, not some artificial calen-

dar scheme, is the catalyst for Divine providence. God is patient, "not wanting any to perish, but all to come to repentance" (2 Pet. 3:9). Jesus was clear that before his return the gospel must go forth into every ethnic group, and we can never know what is fully implied by "the completion of the Great Commission." Who knows but that God is holding back the *parousia* in order to bring in peoples you and I know nothing about. Maybe he is waiting for you or one you love to come into faith!

3. **Get some solid education in eschatological language**. For example, many today use the phrase "the last days" as if this period started a week from last Friday and will end within a few short years. In biblical usage the term "the last days" refers to the period from the coming of the Spirit at Pentecost to the Second Coming of Christ. At Pentecost when Peter quoted the prophet Joel, "In the last days . . . ," we see phenomena that cover both what happened at Pentecost—"I will pour out my Spirit upon all flesh"— and what will occur at the end of the age—"The sun shall be turned to darkness and the moon to blood" (Acts 2:17– 21 [NRSV]). It is all "the last days." We have been in the last days for nearly 2000 years now, and none of us knows whether it will continue on for two years or two thousand years or two million years. Some basic education in apocalyptic literature will go a long way in helping you distinguish good interpretation of the text of Scripture from "holy baloney."

4. **Avoid mixing nationalistic myths with the everlasting gospel of the Kingdom**. Have you noticed how many end-time scenarios give favored status to the United States? Or demonize enemy nations? With the fall of communism the well-worn association of Gog with Russia is no longer viable, and so prophesy preachers are scrambling to find alternatives. Islamic countries are favorite targets. "Is Saddam Hussein the

Antichrist?" is the sort of popular sermon title that is used today. Who will it be tomorrow? I plead with you, do not be a part of this misguided nationalistic fervor.

5. Final counsel is especially directed toward Christian leaders. **Please, for God's sake, refuse to exploit the hopes and fears of your people with speculative prophecy preaching.** Don't weaken the gospel by tickling the ears of your people with the latest apocalyptic scheme. Reckless end-times scenarios have always been counterproductive. They only lead to disillusionment and cynicism. And they discredit the gospel of Jesus Christ. Others may exploit this hot topic for their own gain, but don't you do it. Stay faithful to your calling. Preach Christ risen and present among his people. Preach the kingdom of God here, now, and coming. Make eschatological hope a foundation for faithful living and growing conformity to Christ, not an escape from discipleship. Stoutly refuse to demean the gospel by mixing hope of the Second Coming with reckless speculation.

A TRUSTWORTHY MODEL

In the fourth century, St. Augustine opposed the prophetic literalism of Chiliasm. Instead of the imminent, material, millennial kingdom of Chiliasm, he helped his people see "the City of God." Out of pastoral concern he taught them that the kingdom of God was already a present reality among them in the community of faith and that its full consummation will come in God's time and in God's way in "the blessed hope" of Christ's return. Augustine's wise, sensible biblical vision won the day and influenced the Church for centuries to come. May something of that same faith-filled sensibility arise today.

PEACE AND JOY,
RICHARD J. FOSTER

(Reprinted by permission of Renovare, 8 Inverness Drive East, Suite 102, Englewood, CO 80112-5609)

5.

ANNUAL WORSHIP CALENDAR

Is There Only One Right Way to Worship God?

by Randal G. Dick and J. Michael Feazell

LITURGY HAS BECOME A hot topic in the church these days.
"Excuse me, but what's a liturgy?" you ask.

Liturgy is simply the pattern or program of worship chosen by a church. It includes the gospel-related topics, themes, forms, symbols, styles, seasons and days that help facilitate effective worship for that particular church.

In other words, liturgy refers to the whole set of seasons, days, tools and methods we use to worship, celebrate and enjoy God.

Now we all agree that God doesn't want his people to fight about when to worship him. In fact, all our worship should be a source of unity and joy in the power, love, glory and grace of God.

Yet, so often, our choices about when and how to worship our God and Savior become a source of division and controversy. You know the issues: The Holy Day keepers don't like being in the same church with the Advent Month and Holy Week keepers, and vice versa.

While some members don't mind attending everything the church offers, and some simply avoid the days that are not meaningful to them, others get angry just knowing any ground is being given to the "other side."

In this article, we'd like to present a few basic principles related to worship that might help us all to lay down our weapons and give each other some space about when we choose to worship our great God who loves us all.

WORSHIP IS CELEBRATION

The first thing that might help us get some perspective is to understand that worship is a human response to God—who he is, what he has done and what he is doing. It is an active, often spontaneous celebration of God's work through Christ. In worship Christians are participating in Christ's work of human redemption.

New Testament liturgy is the recurring patterns of worship that developed among the first-century Christians. It developed as the disciples rehearsed and remembered Jesus' death and resurrection by meeting together to participate in the Lord's Supper and to baptize new converts.

These events were discussed, read about in the Scriptures, rehearsed and reenacted in an atmosphere of prayer, singing of hymns, thanksgiving and praise.

GOD LIKES VARIETY

As we learn to obey Jesus' command to love one another, we also learn to appreciate and respect our cultural diversity. Jesus values human culture and human customs because he values humanity.

Our cultural lenses, as it were, are a necessary part of who we are. Consequently, the forms or styles we prefer for worship are necessarily shaped by our particular culture, and rightly so.

As we view life through our particular cultural lenses, we tend to look upon other ways of doing things with suspicion, distrust, ridicule or even fear. Our culture tends to shape our values, and our values govern how we draw our conclusions about what is good and what is bad.

When we come to faith in Christ, God purifies our hearts. He softens our hearts toward others. He gives us a new commandment—that we love one another.

To love one another does not require that we must abandon our unique cultural values. It means we must learn to respect the cultural values of others, without feeling threatened ourselves.

Of course, if a particular cultural value is sinful, we must abandon it. But most of our cultural values are not sinful; many are neutral, and many are quite compatible with godliness in Christ.

CULTURE AND SIN

Culture, of itself, is not evil. Our unity in Christ affirms and purifies culture; it does not do away with it! When Jesus returns, we are told in Revelation, men and women from every tribe and tongue and people and nation will form the kingdom of God.

God works with us in the context of our respective cultures. He is the author of human freedom, and he enjoys the rich tapestry of human diversity and cultural variety. God hates sin, but he does not hate culture.

It is sin that corrupts and spoils culture, not culture that causes and produces sin. Because there is sin in every human, there is sin in every culture. As God's people, Christians should turn away from sin in their respective cultures, but they do not need to turn away from their culture to embrace someone else's culture.

At the same time, no particular cultural form is an absolute. In other words, we must not think that just because a cultural form we especially like is not sinful and has a certain value in worship, therefore it must be used in worship at all costs. To make any cultural form essential to worship is to make the opposite mistake from discarding all cultural forms.

We must be free to use cultural forms in worship, while also remaining free not to use a particular cultural form. We must not allow any form or style of worship to become an end in itself. We worship God, freely using forms and styles of worship; we don't, however, allow ourselves to become slaves to those forms and styles.

COMMUNING WITH GOD

Silly as it sounds to have to say it, God is just as comfortable communing with Filipinos in a Philippine culture as he is communing with Arabs in an Arab culture, Indians in an Indian culture, Danes in a Danish culture, Mexicans in a Mexican culture or Latinos, Anglos, African Americans or American-born Chinese in a United States culture. And God loves the worship of his people regardless of its cultural flavor and style.

Our congregations do not need to have the same songbooks, the same musical instruments, the same style of body movement or even the same days on which we worship in order to be united in Christ. Our unity comes from our faith in Jesus Christ and our mutual love for one another, not from worshiping in the same way and at the same times in every congregation around the world.

Each culture may have different symbols that are meaningful to them. In many cultures, for example, the cross is a fitting symbol of Christian faith, while in certain other cultures it may not be, because of its widespread use in that culture as a symbol of something else.

In many cultures, the Christmas season is a fitting celebration of the birth of Christ, while in certain other cultures it is not, because it has become so entrenched with local spiritism rituals.

LITURGY AND CULTURE

As a congregation matures, it develops an increasingly deeper participation in the Incarnation of Christ through its worship and liturgy. That means the members of the congregation are growing in love for God and in love for others. And that means they are becoming less and less likely to condemn others for being different and for doing things differently.

It should be obvious that the more we love God, and the more we worship and honor him, the less we would tend to condemn our brothers and sisters in Christ who prefer to worship him on days and in ways different from those we choose.

But it isn't obvious, is it? We tend to condemn it anyway. And Christians always have. Less than 25 years after Jesus' death, Paul addressed this issue in his letter to the Romans.

"Who are you to judge someone else's servant? To his own master he stands or falls," Paul writes. "And he will stand, for the Lord is able to make him stand" (Romans 14:4).

Such instructions are necessary for the very reason that Christians do tend to have a spirit of condemnation toward others. Paul continues in verse 10: "You, then, why do you judge your brother? Or why do you look down on your brother? For we will all stand before God's judgment seat."

What does this have to do with liturgy? Just this: We must learn not to condemn one another over the seasons and days on which we decide to worship.

For example, if a congregation in the United States decides to worship on Sunday, then congregations in Europe and South America do not need either to (1) feel they must immediately do the same thing, or (2) get angry and upset that the U.S. congregation has made this decision.

Likewise, if a congregation in South America feels it should not get involved in local Christmas customs, then congregations in the United States and Canada do not have to feel their South American brothers and sisters are being disloyal to Christ.

FREEDOM NOT TO CONDEMN

We are all free in Christ to worship during whatever seasons and on whatever days we find fitting and appropriate.

As Paul wrote to the church in Rome: "He who regards one day as special, does so to the Lord. He who eats meat, eats to the Lord, for he gives thanks to God; and he who abstains, does so to the Lord and gives thanks to God" (Romans 14:6).

Can we let this principle rule our attitudes toward one another? If our brothers and sisters in other congregations are gathering to worship the Lord, then surely we should not get upset about the particular choice of days on which they do so.

Let's take it one step further. In any given congregation we have fellow believers who want to worship on the seven annual holy days as usual, as well as fellow believers who want to worship during the traditional Christian festival seasons.

How do we treat one another? Are we angry and judgmental? Are we considerate and patient? Do we try to understand and appreciate the feelings of those who differ from us? What is the real value of worshiping on any day at all if the fruit of our worship is judgmentalism and condemnation?

Within the essential and central framework of Christian orthodoxy there is much room for diversity.

We have unity in the worship of the Lord, the faithful observance of the sacraments (the Lord's Supper and baptism) and the faithful proclamation of the Word.

We have diversity in the styles and forms we use in administering the sacraments, proclaiming the Word and worshiping the Lord. The Holy Spirit makes us one in Christ, and our diversity in how we express that unity is a gift of God.

RESPONSIBLE CHOICES

Each congregation in its unique setting in the world must take up its own task, with the help of the Holy Spirit, of filling cultural forms with Christian substance.

Choices about symbols, order of meeting, styles of music and prayer forms, and choices about seasons and days, must be the responsibility of the local congregation under the pastor's guidance within the broad and general guidelines provided by the denomination and the regional offices.

The annual worship calendar of the Worldwide Church of God allows for flexibility. Congregations are free to gather for worship during those seasons and days that are most fitting for their circumstances and situations.

The key is, they are functioning within denominational guidelines (that means there are limitations), and they are not compelled to make the same choices as other Worldwide Church of God congregations (that means there is significant freedom within those limitations). At the same time, congregations are expected to respect the choices made by other congregations.

COMPLICATIONS

We realize these issues are complicated. The fact is, some of our members worship on the annual holy days given to Israel for wrong reasons: they believe it is a sin not to observe them.

Many of these members also believe it is a sin to worship during traditional Christian festivals. They feel sullied or dirtied, as some have put it, having to belong to a church in which there are people who celebrate Easter and Christmas.

They are upset that the Worldwide Church of God no longer forbids or avoids these days that they continue to view as sinful, and some of them are praying that God will put everything back the way it used to be.

However, there are others who worship on the seven annual holy days simply because it is their tradition and custom. They associate pleasant memories with the festivals. They are glad they can worship Christ in a new and meaningful way and see their holy day tradition as one means to that end.

Still others have completely redefined the holy days as an especially relevant way to celebrate Christ.

On the other side of the issue are those who do not want to belong to a church that holds any kind of meeting on the Israelite holy days.

Many of these have a keen sense of having been freed from the legalism that characterized the way our church understood these holy days, and they want to steer completely clear of them.

They cannot understand why the church would continue to allow for worship on these days when their observance was a major source of our spirit of exclusivity and our misunderstanding of the gospel.

Others don't mind the church having meetings on the holy days, as long as attendance is not mandatory and as long as meetings are also held during the traditional Christian seasons.

Others do not plan to remain with the Worldwide Church of God if it continues to permit worship on the annual Israelite holy days.

OUR LITURGICAL CALENDAR

These factors and others like them make the liturgical calendar a hot topic indeed. There is no solution that will please everyone.

The goals of the Advisory Council of Elders, the international regional directors and the U.S. regional pastors in formulating a denominational position paper on the annual worship calendar are (1) faithfulness to God, and (2) denominational unity in the light of his Word.

That is why the calendar provides flexibility within an overall biblical framework. Congregations will be free to formulate their own local liturgical calendar within this denominational framework, taking into account the needs and preferences of all the members.

Whether we can handle such freedom is yet to be seen. Can we have diversity in this way and yet remain united in our faith in Jesus Christ and in the fellowship of the Holy Spirit? Surely we can. Whether we will is a matter of choice.

God loves all his children, but his children still struggle with the challenges of working together in love.

May we join together in prayer that as we assemble for worship God will lead us into a closer walk with him and with one another.

(Reprinted by permission from *The Worldwide News,* August 1998)
Randal G. Dick is superintendent of missions
for the Worldwide Church of God.

6.

SIGNIFICANT DATES FOR THE
WORLDWIDE CHURCH OF GOD

1933–34 Herbert Armstrong begins Radio Church of God, *The World Tomorrow* radio program, and *The Plain Truth* magazine

1947 Armstrong moves the ministry to Pasadena, CA, and opens Ambassador College

1950s *The World Tomorrow* begins airing in Europe, Australia, the Philippines, and South Africa, and churches are begun in each region

1960 Ambassador College opens campus in Bricket Wood, England

1964 Ambassador College opens campus in Big Sandy, TX

1968 Radio Church of God becomes Worldwide Church of God

1960s Literature outreach and pastoral ministry begin in Spanish, French, Dutch, and German languages

1978 English campus of Ambassador College closes

1979 State of California imposes receivership, finds no illegalities, drops case

1986 Death of Herbert Armstrong; Joseph W. Tkach appointed pastor general of the church

1992 Church reaches peak worldwide membership of 99,000 with 133,000 in attendance

1993–95   After major doctrinal changes, membership and finances drop sharply; *The World Tomorrow* television program is canceled

1995   Death of Joseph W. Tkach; Joseph W. Tkach Jr. is appointed pastor general of the church

1996   Plain Truth Ministries launched as transdenominational Christian ministry

1997   Ambassador University closes; Worldwide Church of God becomes member of National Association of Evangelicals

Address of world headquarters: Worldwide Church of God, Pasadena, CA 91123. email: info@wcg.org. Website: www.wcg.org

7.

WORLDWIDE CHURCH OF GOD
"Summary of Our Christian Faith"

WE BELIEVE:

In one holy, loving, all-powerful, and gracious Creator God who exists in three Persons: Father, Son, and Holy Spirit.

That the Bible is the inspired and infallible Word of God, fully authoritative for all matters of faith and practice.

That Jesus Christ, born of the virgin Mary, fully God and fully human, is both Lord and Savior.

That Jesus Christ suffered and died on the cross for human sin, that he was raised bodily on the third day, and that he ascended to heaven and sits at the right hand of God the Father.

That Jesus Christ will come again to judge the living and the dead and to reign over all things.

In the Holy Spirit, who brings sinners to repentance, who gives eternal life to believers, and who lives in them to conform them to the image of Jesus Christ.

That Christians should gather in regular fellowship and live lives of faith that make evident the good news that humans enter the kingdom of God by putting their trust in Jesus Christ.

In the spiritual unity of all believers in our Lord Jesus Christ.

That salvation comes not by works, but only by God's grace through faith in Jesus Christ.

In the resurrection of the dead and the life of the world to come.

BIBLIOGRAPHY

Allen, J. H. *Judah's Sceptre and Joseph's Birthright*. Boston: A. A. Beauchamp Publishing Company, 1917.

Armstrong, Herbert W. *The Autobiography of Herbert W. Armstrong*. Pasadena, Calif.: Ambassador College Press, 1973.

_____. *The Book of Revelation Unveiled at Last*. Pasadena, Calif.: Ambassador College Press, 1959.

_____. *Has Time Been Lost?* Pasadena, Calif.: Ambassador College Press, 1952, 1962.

_____. *The Incredible Human Potential*. Pasadena, Calif.: Worldwide Church of God, 1978.

_____. "Is Hitler Alive?" *The Plain Truth* (September 1948): 7.

_____. *Just What Do You Mean—Born Again?* Pasadena, Calif.: Radio Church of God, 1962.

_____. "Just What Is the Christian Church?" Reprint 572. Originally published in *Tomorrow's World* (May 1970): 4.

_____. *Mystery of the Ages*. New York: Dodd, Mead, 1985.

_____. "Personal from Herbert W. Armstrong: Shall We All Leave the Church of God and Join the Church of People?" *The Good News* (September 1980): 26.

_____. *The Tongues Question*. Pasadena, Calif.: Radio Church of God, 1957.

_____. *The United States and British Commonwealth in Prophecy*. Pasadena, Calif.: Ambassador College Press, 1967.

_____. *Which Day Is the Christian Sabbath?* Pasadena, Calif.: Ambassador College Press, 1964, 1968.

_____. ed. *The Ambassador College Bible Correspondence Course, Lesson 19.* Pasadena, Calif.: Ambassador College, 1961.

_____. ed. *The Ambassador College Bible Correspondence Course, Lesson 28.* Pasadena, Calif.: Ambassador College, 1961.

_____. ed. *The Ambassador College Bible Correspondence Course, Lesson 45.* Pasadena, Calif.: Ambassador College, 1966.

Baille, John. *A Diary of Private Prayer.* Springdale, Pa.: Whitaker House, 1979.

Beckham, William A. *The Second Reformation.* Houston, Tex: Touch Publications, 1995.

Bell, Chip. *Managers as Mentors.* San Francisco: Berrett-Koehler Publishers, 1996.

Bonhoeffer, Dietrich. *Life Together.* New York: HarperCollins, 1954.

Boraker, Robert. "The Truth About Drugs and Vaccines." *The Good News* (August 1961): 8.

Buechner, Fredrick. *Telling the Truth: The Gospel as Tragedy, Comedy, and Fairy Tale.* San Francisco: HarperSanFrancisco, 1977.

Caussade, Jean-Pierre de. *The Sacrament of the Present Moment.* Trans. Kitty Muggeridge. New York: Harper and Row, 1982.

Colson, Charles. *The Body: Being Light in the Darkness.* Dallas: Word, 1992.

Crabtree, Davida Roy. *The Empowering Church: How One Congregation Supports Lay People's Ministry in the World.* Washington, D.C.: Alban Institute, 1989.

Dawn, Marva J. *Reaching Out Without Dumbing Down.* Grand Rapids: Eerdmans, 1995.

DePree, Max. *Leadership Is an Art.* New York: Doubleday, 1992.

Easum, William M. *Sacred Cows Make Gourmet Burgers.* Nashville: Abingdon, 1995.

Elliston, Edgar J., and J. Timothy Kauffman. *Developing Leaders for Urban Ministries.* New York: Peter Lang, 1993.

Foster, Richard J. *Celebration of Discipline*. New York: Harper-Collins, 1978, 1988.

_____. "Deepening Our Conversation with God: An Interview with Henri Nouwen and Richard Foster." *Leadership* (Winter 1997): 117–18.

_____. Heart to Heart: A Pastoral Letter from Richard J. Foster." November 1995.

_____. "Spiritual Formation." Lecture at Azusa Pacific University, 14 January 1997.

Fowler, James. *Stages of Faith*. San Francisco: HarperCollins, 1981.

Gaddy, C. Welton. *The Gift of Worship*. Nashville: Broadman, 1992.

Gangel, Kenneth O. "The Pastor as a Motivator." Lecture at Azusa Pacific University, 7 January 1998.

_____. "The Pastor as Planner and Goal Achiever." Lecture at Azusa Pacific University, 6 January 1998.

_____. *Team Leadership in Christian Ministry*. Chicago: Moody Press, 1997.

Gibbs, Eddie. *In Name Only*. Wheaton, Ill.: Victor Books, 1994.

Greenleaf, Robert K. *Servant Leadership*. Mahwah, N.J.: Paulist Press, 1977.

Hayford, Jack. "The Character of a Leader." In *Leaders on Leadership*, ed. George Barna. Ventura, Calif.: Regal Books, 1997.

Hoeh, Herman. *A True History of the True Church*. Pasadena, Calif.: Radio Church of God, 1959.

Internet. *http://anago.wwa.com/~curadist/ReferenceLibrary/Christianity/WCG/bach2.htm*, 8 September 1997, 9:56 a.m.

Johnson, Ben Campbell. *Pastoral Spirituality: A Focus for Ministry*. Philadelphia: Westminster, 1988.

Kaiser Jr., Walter. *Back Toward the Future*. Grand Rapids: Baker, 1989.

Kelly, Thomas. *A Testament of Devotion*. New York: HarperCollins, 1992.

Kempis, Thomas à. *The Imitation of Christ*. Trans. William C. Creasy. Notre Dame, Ind.: Ave Maria Press, 1989.

Kraemer, Hendrick. *A Theology of the Laity*. Philadelphia: Westminster, 1958.

Laubach, Frank. *Man of Prayer*. Syracuse, N.Y.: Laubach Literary International, 1990.

L'Engle, Madeleine. *A Stone for a Pillow*. Wheaton, Ill.: Harold Shaw Publishers, 1956.

Lewis, C. S. *The Last Battle*. New York: Macmillan, 1956.

Lewis, Phillip V. *Transformational Leadership: A New Model for Total Church Involvement*. Nashville: Broadman & Holman, 1996.

Lucado, Max. "A Forgiving Heart." *Preaching* (September-October 1998): 29.

Malphurs, Aubrey. *Developing a Vision for Ministry in the Twenty-first Century*. Grand Rapids: Baker, 1992.

Meredith, Roderick C. *The Inside Story of the World Tomorrow Broadcast*. Pasadena, Calif.: Ambassador College Press, 1963.

Murray, Andrew. *With Christ in the School of Prayer*. Springdale, Pa.: Whitaker House, 1981.

Nee, Watchman. *The Prayer Ministry of the Church*. New York: Christian Fellowship Publishers, 1973.

Nouwen, Henri. "Deepening Our Conversation with God: An Interview with Henri Nouwen and Richard Foster." *Leadership* (Winter 1997): 117–18.

_____. *The Genesee Diary*. New York: Doubleday, 1976.

Ogden, Greg. *The New Reformation: Returning the Ministry to the People of God*. Grand Rapids: Zondervan, 1990.

Sample, Tex, *U. S. Lifestyles and Mainline Churches: A Key to Reaching People in the 90's*. Louisville: John Knox, 1990.

Snyder, Howard A. *Signs of the Spirit*. Eugene, Ore.: Wipf & Stock, 1989.

Stokes, Kenneth. *Faith Is a Verb: Dynamics of Adult Faith Development*. Mystic, Conn.: Twenty-Third Publications, 1994.

Stone, Paul R. *The Caring Church: A Guide for Lay Pastoral Care.* Grand Rapids: Zondervan, 1990.

Temple, William. *Christianity and the Social Order.* New York: Seabury, 1977. Quoted in *Devotional Classics,* ed. Richard J. Foster and James Bryan Smith. San Francisco: HarperSanFrancisco, 1993.

Tkach Sr., Joseph W. "Personal Letter." *Pastor General's Report,* 15 May 1990.

_____. "Personal Letter." *Pastor General's Report,* 28 May 1990.

Tkach, Joseph. *Transformed by Truth.* Sisters, Oreg.: Multnomah, 1997.

Torrance, Thomas F. *The Mediation of Christ.* Colorado Springs, Colo.: Helmers & Howard, 1992.

Tozer, A. W. *The Pursuit of God.* Camp Hill, Pa.: Christian Publications, 1982.

Underhill, Evelyn. *Worship.* Guildford, Surrey, Great Britain: Eagle, 1991.

Webber, Robert E. *Worship Old and New.* Grand Rapids: Zondervan, 1994.

White, James F. *A Brief History of Christian Worship.* Nashville: Abingdon, 1993.

Willard, Dallas. *The Divine Conspiracy.* San Francisco: HarperSanFrancisco, 1998.

_____. *The Spirit of the Disciplines.* San Francisco: HarperCollins, 1988.

Worldwide Church of God. *Vision 2000.* A quad-fold editorial resource provided for pastors of the Worldwide Church of God, published by denominational headquarters, 1997.

Yancey, Philip. "The Holy Inefficiency of Henri Nouwen." *Christianity Today* (9 December 1996): 80.

_____. *The Jesus I Never Knew.* Grand Rapids: Zondervan, 1996.

NOTES

CHAPTER 1—A CRACK IN THE DAM

1. Charles Colson, *The Body: Being Light in the Darkness* (Dallas: Word, 1992). This and other quotes in the next few paragraphs are from page 73.

2. Ambassador College was founded in 1947 by Herbert Armstrong primarily to train ministers and workers for his church. When it closed in 1997 due to lack of adequate funding, it had become a regionally accredited four-year liberal arts university.

3. Herbert W. Armstrong, *Just What Do You Mean—Born Again?* (Pasadena, Calif.: Radio Church of God, 1962), 3.

4. "Statement of Purpose and Rules of Order," Internal memorandum to members of the Worldwide Church of God Doctrinal Manual Group, 18 January 1990.

5. "Doctrinal Manual Materials," Internal memorandum to members of the Worldwide Church of God Doctrinal Manual Group.

CHAPTER 2—A VOICE IN THE WILDERNESS

1. Herbert W. Armstrong, *The Autobiography of Herbert W. Armstrong* (Pasadena, Calif.: Ambassador College Press, 1973), 286.

2. Ibid., 295.

3. Armstrong virtually copied Allen's book, *Judah's Sceptre and Joseph's Birthright* (Boston: A. A. Beauchamp Publishing Company, 1917), in his *The United States and British Commonwealth in Prophecy* (1967).

4. Armstrong commonly claimed these teachings were "revealed by God" to him so that he might preach them to the whole world in preparation for the soon return of Jesus Christ. He often neglected to mention that the "revelations" came through his studies of the theories of other writers; hence, many if not most members of his church believed God had revealed these doctrines personally and directly to him as he studied the Scriptures.

5. Malachi 4:5–6 reads: "Lo, I will send you the prophet Elijah before the great and terrible day of the LORD comes. He will turn the hearts of parents to their children and the hearts of children to their parents, so that I will not come and strike the land with a curse" (NRSV).

6. Herbert W. Armstrong, "Is Hitler Alive?" *The Plain Truth* (September 1948): 7.

7. By late 1928, Armstrong had become convinced that the same rationale that "proved" that the seventh-day Sabbath was binding on Christians also proved that the annual holy days of Leviticus 23 are binding on Christians. Based on his interpretations of Colossians 2:16, Armstrong concluded (rightly) that the Saturday Sabbath and the annual holy days "stand or fall together."

8. Armstrong, *Autobiography*, 287–88. (Note: Armstrong's emphases are retained throughout in quotations of his works and WCG literature.)

9. Ibid., 300.

10. Ibid., 300–302.

11. Herbert W. Armstrong, ed., *The Ambassador College Bible Correspondence Course*, Lesson 19 (Pasadena, Calif.: Ambassador College Press, 1961), 8.

12. Roderick C. Meredith, *The Inside Story of the World Tomorrow Broadcast* (Pasadena, Calif.: Ambassador College, 1963), 47.

13. Herbert W. Armstrong, *The Incredible Human Potential* (Pasadena, Calif.: Worldwide Church of God, 1978), 80–82.

14. Eddie Gibbs, *In Name Only* (Wheaton, Ill.: Victor Books, 1994), 88–98.

15. A. W. Tozer, *The Pursuit of God* (Camp Hill, Pa.: Christian Publications, 1982), 50.

16. Herbert Armstrong's son, the gifted radio and television evangelist Garner Ted Armstrong, had been the "heir apparent" until his father fired and disfellowshiped him for the last time in 1978. The younger Armstrong founded his own ministry that year and has had no association or relationship with the Worldwide Church of God since.

CHAPTER 3—LIGHT SHINES IN MY DARKNESS

1. Herbert W. Armstrong, *The Autobiography of Herbert W. Armstrong* (Pasadena, Calif.: Ambassador College Press, 1973): 318.

2. Robert Boraker, "The Truth About Drugs and Vaccines," *The Good News* (August 1961): 8.

3. In the Worldwide Church of God, Jeremiah 10:1–4 was often cited as a direct biblical condemnation of the Christmas tree. By the mid-1970s, however, the church realized that the passage had reference to wood-crafted idols, and not to decorated pine trees.

CHAPTER 4—"THE ONLY TRUE CHURCH"

1. Herbert W. Armstrong, "Just What Is the Christian Church?" Reprint 572. Originally published in *Tomorrow's World* (Pasadena, Calif.: Ambassador College Press, 1970): 4.

2. Herbert W. Armstrong, "Personal from Herbert W. Armstrong: Shall We All Leave the Church of God and Join the Church of People?" *The Good News*, (September 1980): 26.

3. Kenneth Stokes, *Faith Is a Verb: Dynamics of Adult Faith Development* (Mystic, Conn.: Twenty-Third Publications, 1994), 34.

4. Ibid., 32.

5. Andrew Murray, *With Christ in the School of Prayer* (Springdale, Pa.: Whitaker House, 1981), 192.

6. Ibid., 108.

7. Thomas à Kempis, *The Imitation of Christ*, trans. William C. Creasy (Notre Dame, Ind.: Ave Maria Press, 1989), 30.

8. Armstrong, "Personal," 26.

9. Herbert W. Armstrong, *The Incredible Human Potential* (Pasadena, Calif.: Worldwide Church of God, 1978), 116.

10. Ibid., 118–19.

11. Frank Laubach, *Man of Prayer* (Syracuse, N.Y.: Laubach Literary International, 1990), 250.

12. Thomas à Kempis, *The Imitation of Christ*, 32.

13. Laubach, *Man of Prayer*, 284–85.

CHAPTER 5—A CASE OF MISTAKEN IDENTITY

1. Jesus taught in John 13:35: "By this everyone will know that you are my disciples, if you have love for one another" (NRSV).

2. The essential content of Christian belief is summarized by Jesus in Luke 24:46–48: "Thus it is written, that the Messiah is to suffer and to rise from the dead on the third day, and that repentance and forgiveness of sins is to be proclaimed in his name to all nations, beginning from Jerusalem. You are witnesses of these things" (NRSV). It is also summarized by Paul in 1 Corinthians 15:3–5: "For I handed on to you as of first importance what I in turn had received: that Christ died for our sins in accordance with the scriptures, and that he was buried, and that he was raised on the third day in accordance with the scriptures" (NRSV). The gospel focuses on two fundamental issues that are historical events: Jesus died, and Jesus rose. And this was done for the salvation of all who believe.

3. Adapted from Robert E. Webber, *Worship Old and New* (Grand Rapids: Zondervan, 1994), 75.

4. Ibid., 67.

5. Herbert W. Armstrong, *Which Day Is the Christian Sabbath?* (Pasadena, Calif.: Ambassador College Press, 1964, 1968), 87–88.

6. Ibid., 90.

7. Ibid., 93–94.

8. Herbert W. Armstrong, *Has Time Been Lost?* (Pasadena, Calif.: Ambassador College Press, 1952, 1962), 4.

9. Herman Hoeh, *A True History of the True Church* (Pasadena, Calif.: Radio Church of God, 1959), 29.

10. Ibid.

11. Ibid.

12. Garner Ted Armstrong, son of Herbert, was the voice of *The World Tomorrow* and executive vice president of the church until his father disfellowshipped and ousted him in 1978.

13. Hoeh, *True History*, 29–30.

14. Armstrong's half-hour radio program, which blanketed the country during the decades of the 1950s and 1960s.

15. Hoeh, *True History*, 30.

16. C. Welton Gaddy, *The Gift of Worship* (Nashville: Broadman, 1992), xvii.

17. Frederick Buechner, *Telling the Truth: The Gospel as Tragedy, Comedy, and Fairy Tale* (San Francisco: HarperSanFrancisco, 1977), 7.

18. Ibid., 98.

19. James F. White, *A Brief History of Christian Worship* (Nashville: Abingdon, 1993), 179.

20. Ibid.

21. Ibid.

22. Ibid., 180.

23. Cf. appendix 5, Annual Worship Calendar: Is There Only One Way to Worship God?

CHAPTER 6 — "FOUR TO SEVEN SHORT YEARS"

1. Herbert W. Armstrong, *The United States and British Commonwealth in Prophecy* (Pasadena, Calif.: Ambassador College Press, 1967), ix.

2. Walter Kaiser Jr., *Back Toward the Future* (Grand Rapids: Baker, 1989), 10.

3. Armstrong, *United States and British Commonwealth*, 75.

4. Ibid., 4.

5. Ibid., xii. This version of Armstrong's book was published in 1967. The references to "four to seven years" were, of course, removed in later reprintings. When his book *Mystery of the Ages* was published in 1985, Armstrong, who had not lost confidence in his work, wrote in its introduction, "Time may prove this to be the most important book written in almost 1,900 years."

6. Richard Foster, "Renovare: Heart to Heart, A Pastoral Letter From Richard J. Foster," November 1995. (For the complete text of Richard Foster's letter, see appendix 4.)

7. Joseph W. Tkach Sr., "Personal Letter," *The Pastor General's Report*, 15 May 1990, 3.

8. Joseph W. Tkach Sr., "Personal Letter," *The Pastor General's Report*, 28 May 1990, 4.

9. Armstrong, *United States and British Commonwealth*, 32.

10. The lion's share of Armstrong's book *The United States and British Commonwealth in Prophecy* was lifted virtually verbatim from a book by J. H. Allen, *Judah's Scepter and Joseph's Birthright* (Boston: A. A. Beauchamp Publishing Company, 1917). Although Armstrong often claimed that this "amazing" truth was revealed to him by God, he neglected to add the fact that the "revelation" came through Allen's book.

11. Herbert W Armstrong, *First Corinthians Bible Study Series: Chapter 7*, cassette tape (Pasadena, Calif.: 1980).

12. I am referring specifically to seventh-day Sabbatarianism. However, I believe the principles of legalism apply also to first-day Sabbatarianism.

13. A favorite Armstrong phrase for expressing the simplicity of the truth.

14. Despite the poor research skills of certain cult-watchers, Herbert Armstrong did not deny the divinity of Jesus Christ. At times he unwittingly described the humanity of Jesus in ways

that were logically inconsistent with the divinity of Jesus. Despite this, Armstrong was quite dogmatic about the eternal divinity both of the Father and of the One who became incarnate as Jesus Christ.

15. Madeleine L'Engle, *A Stone for a Pillow* (Wheaton, Ill.: Harold Shaw Publishers, 1956), 68–70.

16. Thomas F. Torrance, *The Mediation of Christ* (Colorado Springs: Helmers & Howard, 1992), 94–95.

CHAPTER 7—THE PAIN OF CHANGE

1. Kenneth O. Gangel, *Team Leadership in Christian Ministry* (Chicago: Moody Press, 1977), 206.

2. Cf. appendix 1, Changed Paradigms in the Worldwide Church of God.

3. Jack Hayford, "The Character of a Leader," in *Leaders on Leadership*, ed. George Barna (Ventura, Calif.: Regal Books, 1977), 71.

4. The Worldwide Church of God has experienced major losses of income and membership since the doctrinal changes were initiated. Cf. appendix 2, Highlights of Worldwide Church of God Doctrinal Changes, with appendix 3,Statistical Summary.

5. Internet. *http://anago.wwa.com/~curadist/Reference Lib.rary/Christianity/WCG/bach2.htm*, 8 September 1997, 9:56 A.M.

6. Kenneth O. Gangel, "The Pastor as a Motivator," Lecture at Azusa Pacific University, 7 January 1998.

CHAPTER 8—A CRISIS IN LEADERSHIP

1. Phillip V. Lewis, *Transformational Leadership* (Nashville: Broadman & Holman, 1996), 131.

2. Kenneth O. Gangel, *Team Leadership in Christian Ministry* (Chicago: Moody Press, 1997), 209.

3. Chip Bell, *Managers as Mentors* (San Francisco: Berrett-Koehler Publishers, 1996), 16.

4. Tex Sample, *U. S. Lifestyles and Mainline Churches: A Key to Reaching People in the 90's* (Louisville: John Knox, 1990), 134.

5. Kenneth O. Gangel, "The Pastor as Motivator," Lecture at Azusa Pacific University, 7 January 1998.

6. Cf. appendix 5, Annual Worship Calendar: Is There Only One Right Way to Worship God?

7. Robert K. Greenleaf, *Servant Leadership* (Mahwah, N.J.: Paulist Press, 1977), 21.

8. Ibid.

9. Ibid.

CHAPTER 9—THE PATH OF RENEWAL

1. Howard A. Snyder, *Signs of the Spirit* (Eugene, Ore.: Wipf & Stock, 1989), 271.

2. Ibid., 276–81.

3. Herbert W. Armstrong, *The Book of Revelation Unveiled at Last* (Pasadena, Calif.: Ambassador College, 1959), 46–47.

4. Undergirding all of these, of course, was the church's belief that the Bible is the inspired Word of God and the final authority on all matters of faith and practice. For more on this topic, see Chapter 7.

5. Herbert W. Armstrong, *The Tongues Question* (Pasadena, Calif.: Radio Church of God, 1957), 7.

6. Except for his views on prayer for divine healing and the use of anointed cloths, which do seem to have originated from his contacts with Pentecostals. Cf. Herbert W. Armstrong, *The Autobiography of Herbert W. Armstrong* (Pasadena, Calif.: Ambassador College Press, 1957, 1958, 1960, 1967), 316–17.

7. *Vision 2000* (a quad-fold editorial resource provided for pastors of the Worldwide Church of God published by denominational headquarters in 1997).

8. Greg Ogden, *The New Reformation: Returning the Ministry to the People of God* (Grand Rapids: Zondervan, 1990), 60–61.

9. Ibid., 211.

10. Aubrey Malphurs, *Developing a Vision for Ministry in the Twenty-First Century* (Grand Rapids: Baker, 1992).

CHAPTER 10—STRATEGIES FOR SOUND BODY LIFE

1. Richard Foster, "Deepening Our Conversation with God: An Interview with Henri Nouwen and Richard Foster," *Leadership* (Winter 1997): 117.

2. Thomas à Kempis, *The Imitation of Christ*, trans. William C. Creasy (Notre Dame, Ind.: Ave Maria Press, 1989), 33.

3. Dietrich Bonhoeffer, *Life Together* (New York: Harper-Collins, 1954), 35–36.

4. Ibid., 36.

5. Herbert W. Armstrong, ed., *The Ambassador College Bible Correspondence Course*, Lesson 28 (Pasadena, Calif.: Ambassador College, 1961), 11.

6. Henri Nouwen, "Deepening Our Conversation with God: An Interview with Henri Nouwen and Richard Foster," *Leadership* (Winter 1997): 117–18.

7. Herbert W. Armstrong, ed., *The Ambassador College Bible Correspondence Course*, Lesson 45 (Pasadena, Calif.: Ambassador College, 1966), 10.

8. Ibid., 14.

9. Richard Foster, "Deepening Our Conversation with God," 118.

10. Thomas Kelly, *A Testament of Devotion* (New York: HarperCollins, 1992), 33.

11. Philip Yancey, *The Jesus I Never Knew* (Grand Rapids: Zondervan, 1996), 95.

12. Jean-Pierre de Caussade, *The Sacrament of the Present Moment*, trans. Kitty Muggeridge (New York: Harper and Row, 1982), 18.

13. Ibid., 98.

14. Herbert W. Armstrong, *Mystery of the Ages* (New York: Dodd, Mead, 1985), 241.

THE LIBERATION OF THE WORLDWIDE CHURCH OF GOD

220

15. Ibid., 243.

16. Ibid., 241.

17. Ibid., 244.

18. Yancey, *The Jesus I Never Knew*, 97.

19. For an excellent presentation on Jesus' proclamation of the kingdom of God, see Dallas Willard, *The Divine Conspiracy* (San Francisco: HarperSanFrancisco, 1998).

20. Henri Nouwen, *The Genesee Diary* (New York: Doubleday, 1976), 156.

21. Richard Foster, "Spiritual Formation," Lecture at Azusa Pacific University, 14 January 1997.

22. Nouwen, *The Genesse Diary*, 144.

23. C. S. Lewis, *The Last Battle* (New York: Macmillan, 1956), 161–65.

24. Philip Yancey, "The Holy Inefficiency of Henri Nouwen," *Christianity Today* (9 December 1996): 80.

25. Thomas à Kempis, *The Imitation of Christ*, 134.

26. William Temple, *Christianity and the Social Order* (New York: Seabury, 1977); quoted in *Devotional Classics*, ed. Richard J. Foster and James Bryan Smith (San Francisco: HarperSanFrancisco, 1993), 254.

INDEX

(Numbers in *italics* indicate photographs)